AN EFFECTIVE & SIMPLE JOURNAL PROMPT
PASSIONATELY
DESIGNING & MANIFESTING THE LIFE YOU

UNCOVER, EMBRACE & ALIGN
YOUR INFINITE CREATIVE MAGIC POTENTIAL.
NURTURE YOUR DEEPEST
PASSIONS & DESIRES INTO ABUNDANCE.
GOAL SETTING & LIFE DESIGNING.
THE S.M.A.R.T. GOAL ACHIEVEMENT FORMULA
WITHIN
THE ALIGNING POWER OF
SIMPLE, YET DETAILED,
MOON PHASE & CYCLE PLANNING.
2018 EDITION.

Designed by
Zaeylin Satya

Disclaimer:

DESIGNED TO BE READ FRONT-TO-BACK COMPLETELY, BEFORE BEING PUT TO USE.
SUCCESSFUL MANIFESTATION DEPENDS ENTIRELY ON INDIVIDUAL EFFORT AND THE
COMMITMENT LEVEL HELD. FOR OPTIMAL RESULTS JOURNAL THE PROMPTS
FOR EACH YEAR, EACH LUNAR CYCLE AND EACH LUNAR PHASE
AS WELL AS EACH INDIVIDUAL DAY
TO KEEP YOURSELF ALIGNED.

YOUR RESULTS ARE ENTIRELY IN YOUR CONTROL AND DEPENDENT ON WHAT YOU CHOOSE TO
DO. YOU MUST APPLY YOURSELF IN EACH AND EVERY MOMENT TO GET YOUR OWN DESIRED
RESULTS. YOUR DESCRIPTION FOR BEING YOUR BEST SELF IS DESIGNED BY NO ONE BUT YOU.
DEFINE WHAT THIS MEANS TO YOU AND APPLY YOURSELF IN EACH MOMENT OF THE DAY SO
THAT YOU CAN CONFIRM WITH YOURSELF THAT YOU ARE GIVING YOUR BEST IN EACH
MOMENT. THIS WILL FUEL THE UNIVERSE'S SUPPORTIVE RELATIONSHIP WITH YOU, BRINGING
YOUR DESIRES INTO MANIFESTATION.

Hello, beautiful soul, I am grateful we have been aligned.

THE COMBO:
UNCOVER YOUR PASSIONS
THEN PUT THEM TO USE,
BY YOUR OWN DESIGN,
YOU WILL APPLY THE
S.M.A.R.T. GOAL ACHIEVEMENT FORMULA
IN ALIGNMENT WITH
THE MOON PHASES & CYCLES.
YOUR DESIRES MANIFESTED THROUGH
DEFINING,
DESIGNING
&
A
L
I
G
N
I
N
G

To **feel**,
live,
& radiate
abundance of love and life.

Goddess Life Designer

WHEN YOU MOVE THE UNIVERSE MOVES WITH YOU

This is my own life designer script
which I abide by while journaling & manifesting for my year to come.
This formula resonates with my own life very well. I love that it is a 'designer',
rather than a planner, because that is exactly what I feel when I think about my
goals and my life--

I am passionately designing each moment.

Designed to provide an increase in blissful, beautiful living, deepened goddess energy,
and successful manifestation through the moon cycles.

We will uncover our innermost passions and desires,
then align those passions and desires with the moon phases and cycles,
while also applying the S.M.A.R.T. goal achievement formula.

Desire tracking with the moon,
in alignment with the most successful goal achievement formula today.

This combination conjures an appreciation and acknowledgment of our universe while
looking into the sky and tracking our goals
with bliss & ease,
moment by moment, one day at a time,
to compose each moon cycle and year of this life [waking dream].

We are increasing our comprehension of
truly surrendering to a power greater than ourself,
allowing the universe to move in and manifest our desires into true form,
in alignment with our productive, inspired actions & pure feelings--
which cannot be disguised, but rather
trained & harnessed for manifesting what we each desire.

This is my own Goddess living recipe for things I have spent years learning & applying.
Designed for my self love rituals & life design this year.
As an overflow I am sharing with everyone else.

I am grateful & blessed that I am truly in love with my life design.

Zaeylin Satya

READ ENTIRELY, FROM FRONT TO BACK., DO NOT SKIP AROUND.
THIS GUIDEBOOK IS DESIGNED AS A FORMULA.
YOU MUST FOLLOW THE FORMULA COMPLETELY, EACH DAY,
IN ORDER TO SUCCESSFULLY MANIFEST YOUR OWN DESIRED RESULTS.

IN YOUR JOURNAL,
WRITE IN CORRESPONDANCE WITH
ALL QUESTIONS, PROMPTS & LISTS.
YOU MAY ALSO USE THE SPACES PROVIDED ON SELECT PAGES,
THEY ARE PROVIDED FOR EASY REFLECTION
AS YOU PROGRESSIVELY MANIFEST YOUR DESIRED LIFE DESIGN THIS YEAR.

SET YOUR LONG TERM GOALS USING THE BLUEPRINT FOR MANIFESTING LONG TERM GOALS PAGE

SET YOUR 3, 6 & 9 MONTH GOALS.

FOLLOW THE SPECIFIC NEW MOON PAGE FOR THIS PRESENT DATE IN TIME.

ALWAYS FOLLOW THE CURRENT MOON PHASE.
EACH SPECIFIC MOON CYCLE PAGE PROVIDES DATES FOR WHEN THE 8 PHASES WILL OCCUR,
GUIDING YOU EFFORTLESSLY THROUGH EACH CYCLE..

FOLLOW & COMPLETE EACH OF THE STEPS LISTED ABOVE. THEN,
UTILIZE THE DAILY JOURNALING PAGES EVERY SINGLE DAY IN ORDER TO
SUCCESSFULLY MANIFEST YOUR OWN DESIRED LIFE DESIGN.

'GOD IS LOVE,
& LIVES WITHIN.'
I NOW UNDERSTAND MY BEING,
I AM SIMPLY
GOD COVERED IN SKIN.

THE ART OF CHANGING PERSPECTIVE.
FROM FOCUSING ON THE PHYSICAL REALM AS TRUTH IN DEFINING WHAT IS REAL .. MY REALITY ..
TO HAVING AN AWAKENING OF TRUTH ~ I AM PURE ENERGY, I AM NOT JUST THIS PHYSICAL BODY..
IN MY PUREST FORM I AM NOT VISIBLE TO THE HUMAN EYE ~ AT ALL. I AM CONNECTED TO MY
CREATIVE LIFE SOURCE. I AM CAPABLE OF CREATING THE EXACT LIFE I DESIRE ~ OR SOMETHING EVEN BETTER ~
WITH THE ACKNOWLEDGEMENT THAT MY LIFE SOURCE SUPPORTS ANY & ALL OF MY DESIRES I AM ABLE TO
EMBRACE & IMPLEMENT THIS TRUTH ~ CONSISTENTLY STRENGTHENING MY INNER POWER & EMANATING THE
VIBRATIONAL ENERGY FREQUENCIES I DESIRE TO MANIFEST WITHIN MY LIFE ~ GRATITUDE, TO ALWAYS ATTRACT
MORE & MORE TO BE GRATEFUL FOR IN MY LIFETIME. MORE LOVE, MORE PASSION & MORE BLISS.
THRIVING WITHIN MY OWN PATH OF PASSIONATE BLISS FIRST.
THEN ACCENTUATING LIFE WITH PHYSICAL THINGS
THE WORLD HAS TO OFFER.
I FULLY RECOGNIZE I AM
NOT TAKING THINGS WITH ME WHEN I LEAVE.
IT IS ABOUT THE WORTH I GIVE WHILE
I AM HERE,
AND THE JOY & ADVENTURES I CREATE.
IN GIVING I DO RECEIVE,
MORE THAN I COULD HAVE
THROUGH RECEIVING ALONE.
DESIRES EXPOSE PASSION & BLISS,
PASSION & BLISS NURTURE DESIRES.

CONTENT REFERENCE GUIDE: BY PAGE NUMBER

Goddess Life Designer

PEEK IN AT
THE 5 AGREEMENTS
FROM DON MIGUEL RUIZ
A GROUNDING FORMULA FOR THIS LIFE
[100 YEAR DREAM].

BE IMPECCABLE WITH YOUR WORD:
SPEAK WITH INTEGRITY. SAY ONLY WHAT YOU MEAN. AVOID USING WORDS TO SPEAK AGAINST YOURSELF OR TO GOSSIP ABOUT OTHERS. USE THE POWER OF YOUR WORD IN THE DIRECTION OF TRUTH & LOVE.

DO NOT TAKE ANYTHING PERSONALLY:
NOTHING OTHERS DO IS BECAUSE OF YOU. WHAT OTHERS SAY AND DO IS A PROJECTION OF THEIR OWN REALITY, THEIR OWN DREAM. WHEN YOU ARE IMMUNE TO THE OPINIONS & ACTIONS OF OTHERS, YOU WON'T BE THE VICTIM OF NEEDLESS SUFFERING.

DO NOT MAKE ASSUMPTIONS:
FIND THE COURAGE TO ASK QUESTIONS & TO EXPRESS WHAT YOU REALLY WANT. COMMUNICATE WITH OTHERS AS CLEARLY AS YOU CAN TO AVOID MISUNDERSTANDINGS, SADNESS & DRAMA. WITH JUST THIS ONE AGREEMENT, YOU CAN COMPLETELY TRANSFORM YOUR LIFE.

ALWAYS DO YOUR BEST:
YOUR BEST IS GOING TO CHANGE FROM MOMENT TO MOMENT; IT WILL BE DIFFERENT WHEN YOU ARE HEALTHY AS OPPOSED TO SICK. UNDER ANY CIRCUMSTANCE, SIMPLY DO YOUR BEST, & YOU WILL AVOID SELF-JUDGEMENT, SELF-ABUSE & REGRET.

BE SKEPTICAL, BUT LEARN TO LISTEN:
DO NOT BELIEVE YOURSELF OR ANYBODY ELSE.
USE THE POWER OF DOUBT TO QUESTION EVERYTHING YOU HEAR.
IS IT REALLY THE TRUTH?
LISTEN TO THE INTENT BEHIND WORDS
& YOU WILL UNDERSTAND THE REAL MESSAGE.

YOU COME FIRST.
MAKE CERTAIN TO LOVE YOURSELF, GODDESS

KEEP A LIST OF THINGS YOU LOVE ABOUT
YOURSELF:
ALWAYS ADD TO IT.

KEEP A LIST OF THINGS YOU ARE
GRATEFUL FOR:
ALWAYS ADD TO IT.

TAKE SOME DEEP BREATHS

EAT WELL & HYDRATE

TAKE A WALK

GET IN THE SUN

TAKE A SHOWER

WATCH CLOUDS

GO FOR A DRIVE

JOURNAL

GET A MANICURE/PEDICURE

LISTEN TO MUSIC,
AN AUDIOBOOK
OR A PODCAST

WAKE UP TO WATCH THE SUNRISE

Self Care is Self Love

Self Love is Self Care

APPLY A FACE MASK

LISTEN TO 432 HERTZ OR 528 HERTZ
ON YouTube

GET COSY

GO TO A FARMERS MARKET

BE YOUR PUREST FORM

TAKE A NAP

WATCH SUNSETS

WATCH TUTORIALS ON
YOUTUBE FOR WHAT
INTERESTS YOU

GET A MASSAGE

TAKE A BATH
WITH ESSENTIAL OILS,
DEAD SEA SALT/HIMALAYAN SALT,
CANDLES,
HERBS
& MEDITATION MUSIC/SOUNDS.

GET YOUR BODY MOVING.
OUR BODIES CRAVE MOVEMENT
& RELEASE ENDORPHINS TO ENJOY

READ A BOOK,
OR A BLOG

BRING TEA, LEMON-MINT WATER OR
LEMON-CUCUMBER WATER TO DRINK.

I MOVE MY BODY
BECAUSE I LOVE &
RESPECT MY BODY.

CREATE AN I AM AFFIRMATION TO
REPEAT.

The most fulfilling & abundant feeling
I've ever experienced... I feel that now.
This is how I feel when praying,
meditating & in every other moment
that I remind myself to.

BE ABOUT THE SOLUTION,
NOT THE PROBLEM

ALLOW YOURSELF TO DAY DREAM
& JOURNAL YOUR DAYDREAMING

WATCH A RIVER FLOW

FOLLOW THE LIFE DESIGN PLAN YOU CREATE.
IN EACH MOMENT,
TO CREATIVELY DESIGN EACH DAY,
INTO EACH MONTH & EACH YEAR.

PRAY
THROUGH
GIVING THANKS IN ADVANCE
FOR WHAT YOU DESIRE,
'THANK YOU FOR ____, OR SOMETHING BETTER'
USE SUPERIOR CLARITY IN DESCRIBING THE THINGS WHICH YOU DO DESIRE,
IGNITE ALL YOUR SENSES IN THE FEELING OF THE DESIRE FULFILLED.
TRUST YOUR DESIRES ARE ALREADY BEING FULFILLED.

WEAR WHAT MAKES YOUR
VIBRATION
FEEL BEST

IN SHOWER MEDITATION:

VISUALIZE WASHING AWAY YOUR STRESS
& ANXIETY. CONCENTRATE ON THE FEEL
OF THE WATER UPON YOUR SKIN.
ENVISION THE POWER OF THE WATER
WASHING AWAY YOUR NEGATIVE
THOUGHTS. FEEL SADNESS, REGRET,
ANGER, AND DEPRESSION
WASHING RIGHT OFF YOU.
LET IT ALL GO DOWN THE DRAIN.
FEEL THE LIGHTNESS IN YOUR BODY.
ENJOY THE CLARITY OF YOUR MIND.
YOUR SOUL IS FREE OF ALL THAT DOES
NOT SERVE YOUR HIGHEST GOOD.
YOU ARE READY FOR A NEW BEGINNING.

I'LL BELIEVE IT WHEN I SEE IT,
SWITCHED TO
I'LL SEE IT WHEN I BELIEVE IT.

GO TO BED EARLY

WHO DO I SPEND MY TIME AROUND?
ARE THEY MOTIVATING, OR NOT?
ARE THEIR GOALS/DESIRES ALIGNED WITH MINE?
WHAT IS THEIR ROLE IN MY LIFE?

MEDITATE
TO RECEIVE GUIDANCE,
OBSERVE THOUGHTS & FEELINGS THAT ARISE.
[THEY ARE YOUR INTUITION SPEAKING]

RECOGNIZE, WE EACH CHOOSE
WHAT WE LET IN OUR MINDS AS TRUTH.

DO YOU LET YOUR HIGHER SELF OR
LOWER SELF TALK TO YOU?
ARE YOU SELF-LOVING, OR ARE YOU
SELF-CRITICIZING
WE CHOOSE WHAT WORDS (FROM
BOTH OURSELVES & OTHERS)
WE ALLOW TO
DEFINE OUR DESIGN & TRUTH.

DAILY RITUAL:
MY AFFIRMATION WHENEVER I
LOOK INTO A MIRROR:
I AM BEAUTIFUL,
MY LIFE IS BLISSFUL.

MEDITATION ISN'T
ABOUT GETTING RID OF YOUR THOUGHTS,
IT IS ABOUT OBSERVING THEM
& TRAINING YOURSELF TO
RECOGNIZE YOU CAN
DESIGN THEM IN EACH MOMENT.
RECOGNIZE YOU ARE THINKING [IN THIS MOMENT].
THERE YOU GO, YOU MEDITATED.
PRACTICE NON JUDGEMENT, PURE OBSERVATION OF YOUR THOUGHTS.

Goddess Life Designer

IN MY FREE TIME I FIND MYSELF INTERESTED IN___.

IT IS IMPORTANT TO BE COMPLETELY TRUE TO OUR DESIRES, NOT OTHER PEOPLES, WHEN WE ARE JOURNALING THROUGH THE GODDESS LIFE DESIGNER.

___ IS THE PERSON OUT OF ALL PEOPLE ON THIS PLANET [LIVING, OR NOT] I HAVE COME TO ADMIRE THE MOST. & THIS IS WHY, IN DETAIL:

Goddess Life Designer

___ IS WHAT I HAVE ALWAYS WANTED TO DO SOMEDAY.

S
MY GOAL IS **SPECIFIC, SEXY, SIMPLE, SENSIBLE & SIGNIFICANT**
TO MY LIFE DESIRES.

M
I AM **MOTIVATED** BY MY GOAL, IT IS **MEANINGFUL & MEASURABLE.**

A
I AM **ABLE TO TAKE ACTION** TOWARDS MY GOAL
& I FULLY BELIEVE IT IS **ATTAINABLE.**

R
MY GOAL IS **RESONATING** WELL WITH MY LIFE & DESIRES, IT IS **RELEVANT,**
REALISTIC, THE RESOURCES ARE AVAILABLE TO ME [OR I KNOW HOW I CAN
OBTAIN THEM IN AN APPROPRIATE TIME FRAME]
& IT IS **RESULTS-BASED.**

T
MY GOAL IS **TIME** BASED, **TIMELY, TIME** SENSITIVE, **TIME** LIMITED
& AIMED **TOWARDS** DESIRES.

Goddess Life Designer
SINCE THE S.M.A.R.T. GOAL METHOD IS ACTING WITHIN EACH LUNAR MONTHS DESIGNING:

It is important we acknowledge that this is a feeling based practice
& what we decide is attainable or realistic will largely depend on
how our own belief system is structured & functioning at this given point in time.
Our highest self must be aware of & in align with that which we desire.
In each moment of each day we are certain
we are acting in accordance with the life design we desire.
The level of faith we hold in the universe contains
a massive amount of power when it comes down to
"what is attainable and realistic",
because, in reality, everything is.
Our beliefs & mindset are what ultimately decide
these two things for our reality around us as we know it.
It is important to have a playful attitude
while mastering our mindset,
we must not throw judgement at ourself.
Always being gentle to ourself.
We are expanding.
We are bursting at the seams with infinite abundance & bliss.
Always believe in yourself.

QUICK REFERENCE THE LUNAR PHASES OF EACH CYCLE

NEW MOON

THIS IS WHEN WE DECIDE WHAT GOAL/DESIRE WE WILL BE MANIFESTING THIS MONTH.

CRESCENT MOON

WE TRULY TAKE TIME TO RELAX & JOURNAL OUR FEELINGS
ON WHAT OUR GOAL/DESIRE **FEELS** LIKE AS MANIFESTED IN OUR LIFE.

FIRST QUARTER MOON

WE WILL TAKE OUR BIG ACTION TOWARD OUR GOAL/DESIRE.
WE CONTINUE TO **FEEL** OUR GOAL/DESIRE AS ALREADY MANIFESTED.

GIBBOUS MOON

WE TAKE TIME TO RELAX & TRUST THAT THE UNIVERSE HAS OUR BACK.
EVERYTHING IS BEING ALIGNED IN PERFECT TIME.
WE CONTINUE TO **FEEL** OUR GOAL/DESIRE AS ALREADY MANIFESTED.

FULL MOON

WE CONTINUE TAKING DAILY INSPIRED ACTION TOWARDS OUR GOAL/DESIRE.
WE CONTINUE TO **FEEL** OUR GOAL/DESIRE AS ALREADY MANIFESTED.

DISSEMINATING MOON

WE RELAX & GIVE GENUINE THANKS
AS OUR GOAL/DESIRE MANIFESTS INTO TRUE FORM.
I AM GRATEFUL THAT EVERYTHING IS IN ALIGNMENT WITH
THE HIGHEST GOOD FOR ALL.

THIRD QUARTER MOON

WE GIVE BACK NOW, AS WE HAVE ABUNDANTLY MANIFESTED OUR GOAL/DESIRE
INTO OUR LIFE.
THIS IS A GREAT TIME FOR
[EXTRA] SELF LOVE RITUALS, TO KEEP US INSPIRED,
& OUR SELF APPRECIATION GOING STRONG.

BALSAMIC MOON

I AM GRATEFUL
FOR ALL THAT I HAVE ACHIEVED & RECEIVED.
I AM FEELING PHENOMENAL & INSPIRED,
AS I RELAX DEEPER INTO MY APPRECIATION, CONFIDENCE, SUCCESS, INFINITE LOVE,
&
ALIGNMENT
WITH THE UNIVERSE.
I AM ALWAYS DIVINELY GUIDED & SUPPORTED.

MEDITATE ON EACH AREA WITHIN YOUR OWN BODY,
INHALE HEALING ENERGY INTO THESE SPACES,
EXHALE ALL THAT DOES NOT SERVE YOUR BEST SELF.

[VIOLET]
CROWN CHAKRA
I AM DIVINE
[THE TOP OF HEAD]
YOUR CONNECTION TO THE DIVINE, UNIVERSE & YOUR SOUL
BLISS
[CENTRAL NERVOUS SYSTEM]

[INDIGO]
3RD EYE CHAKRA
I AM CONNECTED
[ABOVE BROW, CENTERED BETWEEN EYES]
INTUITION & PSYCHIC SENSES
[EYES & PINEAL GLAND]

[BLUE]
THROAT CHAKRA
I AM EXPRESSIVE
COMMUNICATION & PERSONAL TRUTH
[EARS & THROAT]

[GREEN]
HEART CHAKRA
I AM LOVED
LOVE & RELATIONSHIPS
BALANCE
[LUNGS & HEART]

[YELLOW]
SOLAR PLEXUS CHAKRA
I AM STRONG
[ABDOMEN, ABOVE BELLY BUTTON]
CONFIDENCE & PERSONAL POWER
CREATIVITY
[DIGESTIVE SYSTEM]

[ORANGE]
SACRAL CHAKRA
I AM CREATIVE
CREATIVITY, EMOTIONS, & SELF-EXPRESSION
SEXUALITY
[REPRODUCTIVE AREA]

[RED]
ROOT CHAKRA
I AM SAFE
YOUR POWER BASE
CENTERING
[LEGS, SPINE & ADRENAL GLANDS]

ALIGNING HEALING CRYSTALS WITH CHAKRAS IS AS SIMPLE AS
COLOR MATCHING

BEING TRUE TO OURSELVES IS ALWAYS FIRST PRIORITY.
ALLOWING OURSELVES TO ACCEPT THAT WE FEEL NEGATIVITY
IS MUCH BETTER THAN FIGHTING AGAINST IT.
THE PERMITTING OF OUR EMOTIONS IS AN ACT OF SELF LOVE.
RATHER THAN BEING FALSELY OPTIMISTIC WE ARE ACCEPTING, PROCESSING
AND TRANSFORMING OUR EMOTIONS
IN ORDER TO STAY ALIGNED WITH OUR HIGHEST PURPOSE,
IMMERSING DEEPER INTO OUR PASSIONS & BLISS.
ALLOWING OURSELVES TO BE OUR OWN TRUTH.

KEEP YOUR CHAKRAS ALIGNED

I am vibrating within a temple of pure love, covered in skin.

Be conscious when providing fuel & hydration to your temple.
Everything you place into your body should be
the highest of quality.
That which is consumed by the human body holds impact on
energy levels,
emotions, aura and vibration.

Healthy eating can be simple or complex.
Simply, always choose the most pure & whole form
available for each food you desire to consume.

Hydration

Eight 8-ounce glasses,
the same as 2 liters,
or 1 half-gallon of water per day

ENERGY & STAMINA
SUPPLE, CLEAR & GLOWING SKIN
AIDS DIGESTION
PROMOTES CARDIOVASCULAR HEALTH
QUALITY MUSCLE & JOINT FUNCTION
CLEANSES YOUR BODY

THERE IS POWER IN CLEAN & TIDY.

TAKE EXCEPTIONAL CARE OF
YOURSELF
&
YOUR BELONGINGS.
SHOW THE UNIVERSE YOU ARE
GRATEFUL
&
DESERVING
OF YOUR DESIRES.

OPT FOR LESS, IN BETTER QUALITY.
OVER MORE, IN POOR QUALITY.

EXPENSIVE DOES NOT ALWAYS EQUATE TO QUALITY.

SHOULD YOU FIND YOURSELF
OVERWHELMED
BY THE AMOUNT OF BELONGINGS TO CARE FOR
DO DOWNSIZE.
LET GO - KNOW THERE IS AN ABUNDANCE OF EVERYTHING YOU WILL EVER DESIRE.

GIVE!
GIVE AWAY EVERYTHING THAT DOES NOT BRING YOU PURE JOY.
HOLD IT
& **FEEL** WHAT IT BRINGS TO YOU.

CHOOSE TO SURROUND YOURSELF WITH THE THINGS YOU TRULY LOVE ~
DISCARD THE REST.
[ALSO APPLIES TO PEOPLE & PLACES]

GIVE THANKS TO EACH ITEM YOU LET GO OF.
RESPECT THAT AT ONE MOMENT IT DID BRING YOU JOY, EVEN IF THAT WAS ONLY
IN THE MOMENT WHEN YOU PURCHASED IT AND NEVER USED IT.
RELEASE.
ALLOW FOR SPACE TO BE CREATED IN YOUR LIFE FOR MIRACLES TO MANIFEST SIMPLY BY
LETTING GO.

DETACHMENT IS NOT THAT YOU SHOULD OWN NOTHING,
BUT THAT NOTHING SHOULD OWN YOU.
- ALI IBN ABI TALIB

*Be gentle with yourself,
you are doing your best in each moment.*

AS WITH OUR BODIES,
OUR MINDS & MANIFESTING POWERS
DESERVE A WARM UP
BEFORE WE START USING THEM FULL FORCE.

DO THESE 2 THINGS BEFORE DESIGNING YOUR NEW MOON GOALS FOR
EACH CYCLE,
YOUR LONG TERM GOALS
& YOUR 3, 6 & 9 MONTH ALIGNMENT GOALS.

BEGIN BY
STATING YOUR INTENTION
[PRAYER/AFFIRMATION]
ALWAYS IN THE PRESENT TENSE OF YOUR SOLUTION/DESIRE COMPLETELY
MANIFESTED.
EXAMPLE: I AM GRATEFUL FOR ALL OF THE INSIGHT I HAVE RECEIVED IN MY
MEDITATION.
I AM NOW EFFORTLESSLY ABLE TO DEFINE
MY OWN
PASSIONS & DESIRES.
I KNOW THAT IN EACH MOMENT I AM CREATING
MY DESIRED LIFE DESIGN.

THEN RECEIVE
[MEDITATE]
GO TO A PLACE YOU LOVE,
WHERE YOU REALLY **FEEL** YOU ARE YOUR MOST RELAXED, SINCERE SELF.
SOMETIMES YOU WILL RECEIVE INSIGHT OR INTUITION DURING MEDITATION,
OTHER TIMES IT COMES SHORTLY AFTER MEDITATION WHEN YOU ARE STILL
RELAXED.
BUT ACTUALLY,
INSIGHTS & INTUITIONS CAN SINK INTO YOUR MIND AT ANY MOMENT.
DAY OR NIGHT.
THEY ARE THERE WHENEVER YOU DESIRE TO TUNE IN.
CREATE YOUR OWN WAY TO MEDITATE & RECEIVE.

UTILIZE THESE NEXT FEW MEDITATIVE PAGES I HAVE CREATED
&
CREATE YOUR OWN DESIGN WITH SIMILAR STRUCTURE.
I FIND THEM TO BE A VISION BOARD OF WORDS.
CREATE A VISION BOARD OF YOUR OWN,
OR A VISION BOARD SLIDESHOW ON YOUR PHONE,
OUT OF IMAGES REPRESENTING YOUR DESIRES,
SET AN ALARM TO VIEW YOUR IMAGES LEAST ONCE A DAY.

I AM AFFIRMATIONS
USING THE 2 MOST POWERFUL WORDS
TO ASSURE CERTAINTY AND MANIFESTATION

I AM A GODDESS.

I AM WISE.

I AM ALWAYS ABLE TO UNDERSTAND THINGS EASILY.

I AM AWARE AND INTUITIVE.

I AM A MASTER IMPLICATIOR.

I AM ENJOYING EACH AND EVERY MOMENT OF MY LIFE.

I AM ON A BLISSFUL LIFE JOURNEY.

IN EVERY MOMENT I AM UNDERSTANDING
& IN CONTROL OF MY EMOTIONS.

I AM AWARE OF THE DESIGN I AM CREATING EACH MOMENT.

I AM GENTLE WITH MYSELF.

I AM ALWAYS FINDING MYSELF SMILING.

CREATE YOUR OWN I AM AFFIRMATIONS SIMPLY BY PLACING YOUR OWN DESIRES INTO ANY PRESENT TENSE I AM SENTENCE.

REPEAT I AM AFFIRMATIONS TO YOURSELF AT ANY TIME OR USE THEM AS A CONCENTRATION POINT DURING MEDITATION

Goddess Life Designer

IF I SHARE TOO MUCH KNOWLEDGE & WISDOM WITH OTHERS.
I MIGHT LOSE OUT.. BECAUSE THEY WILL ALSO GROW.
THERE ISN'T ENOUGH FOR EVERYONE
TO HAVE EVERYTHING THEY WANT.
[MINDSET OF SCARCITY]

THIS IS SO FALSE
--
THERE IS INFINITE AMOUNTS OF ABUNDANCE
FOR ANY AND EVERY PERSON
TO HAVE EVERYTHING THEY DESIRE,
YOUR ONLY LIMITING FACTOR IN LIFE IS YOU.
SHARING KNOWLEDGE & WISDOM WITH OTHERS
SO THAT THEY CAN ACHIEVE THIER BEST LIFE
IS SO REWARDING & FULFILLING!
[MINDSET OF INFINITE ABUNDANCE]

THE BEST LEADERS LEAVE OTHERS FEELING , 'WE DID IT OURSELVES.' - TAO VERSE 17

Goddess Life Designer

I am infused with love

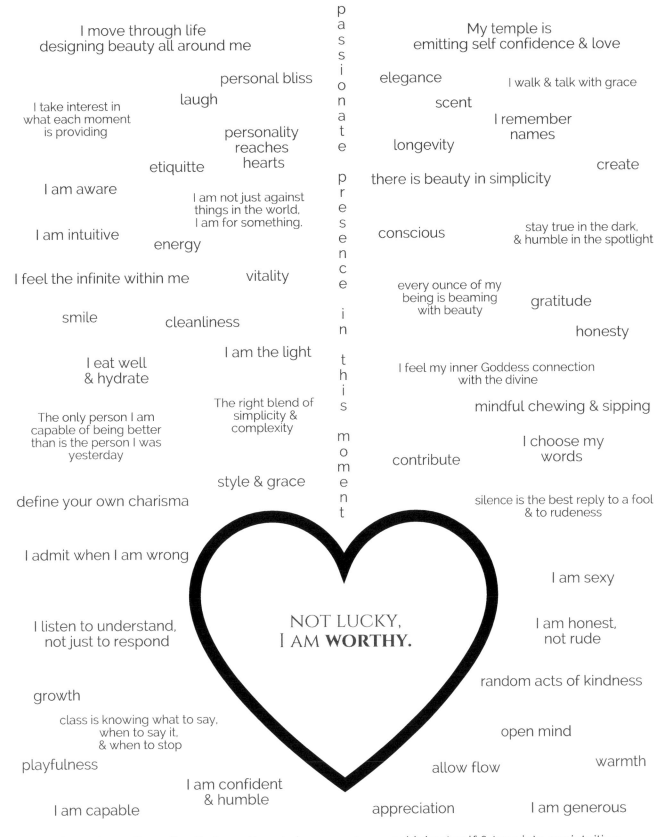

I move through life
designing beauty all around me

My temple is
emitting self confidence & love

p
a
s
s
i
o
n
a
t
e

personal bliss

laugh

elegance

I walk & talk with grace

scent

I take interest in
what each moment
is providing

personality
reaches
hearts

longevity

I remember
names

etiquitte

create

I am aware

there is beauty in simplicity

p
r
e
s
e
n
c
e

I am not just against
things in the world,
I am for something.

I am intuitive

energy

conscious

stay true in the dark,
& humble in the spotlight

I feel the infinite within me

vitality

every ounce of my
being is beaming
with beauty

gratitude

smile

cleanliness

i
n

honesty

I eat well
& hydrate

I am the light

I feel my inner Goddess connection
with the divine

t
h
i
s

The only person I am
capable of being better
than is the person I was
yesterday

The right blend of
simplicity &
complexity

mindful chewing & sipping

I choose my
words

m
o
m
e
n
t

contribute

style & grace

define your own charisma

silence is the best reply to a fool
& to rudeness

I admit when I am wrong

I am sexy

NOT LUCKY,
I AM **WORTHY.**

I listen to understand,
not just to respond

I am honest,
not rude

random acts of kindness

growth

class is knowing what to say,
when to say it,
& when to stop

open mind

playfulness

warmth

allow flow

I am confident
& humble

I am capable

appreciation

I am generous

I am strong & gentle all at one time. I always nurture my highest self & tune into my intuition.

TO FURTHER EXPOSE
YOUR INNERMOST *passions & desires*

I SPEND MY TIME DOING ___ BECAUSE I KNOW, FOR CERTAIN, I ALREADY HAVE ACCESS TO UNLIMITED FINANCIAL ABUNDANCE FOR LIFE.

MEDITATTE ON THESE &/OR SIMILAR QUESTIONS. CREATE YOUR OWN LIST OF QUESTIONS. KEEP REFLECTING BACK, IN ORDER TO STAY ALIGNED.

WRITE DOWN ALL THE DEAILS OF HOW YOU DESIRE YOUR LIFE TO BE IN THESE AREAS:

HEALTH
LOVE
WEALTH

I HAVE MORE THAN I WILL EVER NEED FINICALLY FOR MY ENTIRE LIFETIME. THIS IS HOW I CHOOSE TO GIVE BACK:

_____

I ALWAYS FOLLOW WHAT MAKES ME FEEL GOOD. I KNOW WHAT IS IT ABOUT CERTAIN THINGS THAT MAKES ME FEEL SO GOOD PARTAKING IN THEM. THESE THINGS LISTED:

_____

Goddess Life Designer

Your passions & desires are already inside of you, they always have been.

JOURNAL ON THESE PROMPTS:

I FEEL WARM AND LOVED INSIDE WHEN I AM:

I LOVE LEARNING ABOUT___/ I DESIRE TO KNOW MORE ABOUT___:

ALWAYS KEEP A JOURNAL OF WHAT YOU LEARN.
SHARE YOUR PERSPECTIVE INSIGHTS WITH OTHERS IN ANY WAY YOU DESIRE TO.

IN THE MORNING I AM INSPIRED TO WAKE UP BECAUSE I REMEMBER I AM GOING TO ___ TODAY:

IF I WERE TO SUDDENLY FIND MYSELF AT THE END OF THIS LIFETIME I WOULD HAVE WISHED I HAD THESE EXPERIENCES & ADVENTURES:

Goddess Life Designer

REVIEW ALL YOU HAVE JOURNALED, IN REGARDS TO YOUR PASSIONS & DESIRES.
SIT WITH THESE GOOD FEELINGS FOR A FEW MOMENTS OF BREATHING.

THINK OF THE HAPPIEST MOMENT OF YOUR LIFE,
HOW DID YOU FEEL?
YOU CAN FEEL THAT NOW, RIGHT?
THIS IS THE 'FEELING' STATE YOU WANT TO BE IN
WHILE GOAL SETTING & MANIFESTING.
PASSION [PLUS] GIVING VALUE TO OTHERS = TRUE BLISS & ETERNAL SOUL FULFILLMENT.

20 WRITE DOWN EVERY SINGLE PROBLEM
YOU HAVE WITHIN YOUR LIFE.
BOTH BIG AND SMALL, WRITE THEM ALL.

WRITE DOWN THE IDEAL SOLUTION
TO EACH PROBLEM YOU HAVE LISTED.

NOW, CREATE A PRESENT TENSE THANK YOU STATEMENT FOR EACH IDEAL SOLUTION.
DO SO AS IF IT HAS ALREADY BEEN PERFECTLY ALIGNED WITH & FULLY MANIFESTED INTO YOUR LIFE.
WHAT ARE YOU THANKFUL THE SOLUTION HAS DONE FOR YOU AND YOUR LIFE?

FEEL GOOD WHILE WRITING EACH OF THESE STATEMENTS.
YOUR FEELING STATE CREATES THE VIBRATION YOU ARE EMANATING,
SO CREATE THE VIBRATION YOU DESIRE TO RECEIVE.
EMBODY IT WITHIN YOURSELF FIRST.

WORDS ON THEIR OWN ARE JUST SYMBOLS.

FEEL THE GRATITUDE, JOY AND PEACE THESE STATEMENTS BRING TO YOUR LIFE.
REFER TO THIS LIST OFTEN, ESPECIALLY IF YOU ARE FEELING OVERWHELMED OR DOWN.
IT WILL LIFT YOUR VIBRATION & SPEED UP YOUR MANIFESTATION PROCESS.

FORGIVENESS SETS ME FREE & ALLOWS THE UNIVERSE TO MOVE IN WITH ANY & ALL OF MY DESIRES.

HAND WRITE A LIST ON A SHEET OF PAPER.

LIST EVERY SINGLE THING WITHIN YOUR LIFE THAT NEEDS TO BE FORGIVEN.
THIS MAY INCLUDE SITUATIONS, CIRCUMSTANCES OR OTHER PEOPLE.

**MOST IMPORTANTLY THINK ABOUT
THE FORGIVENESS YOU NEED TO SEND TO YOUR OWN SELF.**

FOR EXAMPLE, THIS MAY INCLUDE FORGIVENESS OF YOUR PAST ACTIONS,
NEGATIVE SELF-TALK OR FINANCIAL DEBT.

YOU CAN **FEEL** THE **PAIN**, THE **HATE**, THE **REGRET**, THE **ANGER**, THE **FEAR**, ALL THE **FEELINGS**
THAT THESE THINGS BRING WHEN THINKING OF THEM.

LIST THEM ALL.

AFTER LISTING EVERY SINGLE THING YOU CAN THINK OF,
GIVE THANKS FOR THE LESSONS OR INSIGHT THAT EACH HAS GIVEN YOU, AND FOR THE CLARITY
YOU HAVE GAINED ON HOW YOU DESIRE THIS SPECIFIC AREA OF YOUR LIFE TO BE.

THIS WILL BE MORE DIFFICULT FOR CERTAIN THINGS THAN OTHERS,
BUT THAT IS ALL THE MORE REASON WHY IT IS IMPORTANT TO DO THIS EXERCISE.

FINANCES CAN BE ESPECIALLY DIFFICULT TO FORGIVE,
BUT YOU MUST BE GRATEFUL FOR THE THINGS AND EXPERIENCES
WHICH YOU HAVE ENJOYED THROUGH YOUR PAST SPENDING.
IN ORDER TO EFFORTLESSLY ATTRACT MORE ABUNDANCE INTO YOUR LIFE
IT IS CRUCIAL TO SPEND MONEY **CHEERFULLY AND GRATEFULLY.**

MAKE SURE THAT YOU ARE NOT CAUGHT UP IN MENTAL FANTASIES OF REVENGE / WISHING NEGATIVITY / FAILURE
ON ANOTHER.. EVER. PERIOD. THE THINKING STATE OF REVENGE PLACES YOU IN A LOW-VIBRATIONAL FREQUENCY
AND WILL NOT IMPACT THE OTHER AT ALL.. EVER. YOUR OWN THOUGHTS, EMOTIONAL FEELINGS & OVERALL
VIBRATIONAL FREQUENCY WILL ONLY EVER IMPACT YOU. THE VIBRATIONS YOU SEND OUT ARE A MATCH FOR THAT
WHICH YOU ARE MANIFESTING WITHIN YOUR LIFE. YOUR POWER OF MANIFESTATION CANNOT BE TURNED OFF,
CHOOSE TO HARNESS IT & DISCIPLINE YOURSELF IN ONLY THINKING ON & FEELING THE VIBRATIONS YOU WISH TO
MANIFEST. THIS ALSO MEANS THAT ANOTHER CANNOT WISH NEGATIVITY OR REVENGE ON YOU --ANY PERSON
FOCUSED ON THE EGOTISTICAL FEELINGS OF REVENGE WILL ONLY ATTRACT THAT VIBRATION TO THEMSELF.

SEND LOVE AND FORGIVENESS TO EACH ITEM ON YOUR LIST
AS YOU WORK THROUGH CROSSING THEM ALL OFF. **PHYSICALLY** CROSS THEM OFF.
IN DOING SO YOU ARE CREATING SPACE WITHIN YOUR MIND
FOR THE UNIVERSE TO MOVE IN AND FULFILL YOUR DESIRED MANIFESTATIONS.

BURN THIS LIST [SAFELY] WHEN YOU ARE FINISHED WITH THE EXERCISE.

IT FEELS AMAZING TO LET GO AND ALLOW YOUR DESIRES TO FLOW IN.

SUBCONSCIOUS LIMITING BELIEFS & YOUR DEFINITION OF SUCCESS

KNOW YOUR PERSONAL DEFINITION OF SUCCESS.

HAVE A WRITTEN COPY OF WHAT SUCCESS MEANS TO YOU, SO THAT YOU CAN REFLECT ON IT WHEN YOU NEED TO. KNOWING WHAT SUCCESS MEANS TO YOU PERSONALLY ALLOWS YOU TO MEASURE HOW CLOSE YOU ARE TO THAT DEFINITION, AND KNOW WHEN YOU HAVE ACHIEVED IT. IT ALSO ALLOWS YOU TO ALIGN EACH AREA OF YOUR LIFE ACCORDINGLY.

ASK YOURSELF:
WHAT WOULD THE VERSION OF MYSELF WHO HAS ACHIEVED MY DEFINITION OF SUCCESS
BE DOING EACH DAY THAT I AM NOT DOING IN MY LIFE PRESENTLY?
WHAT WOULD THIS SUCCESSFUL VERSION OF MYSELF NOT BE DOING ANYMORE THAT I AM PRESENTLY DOING?

MAKE A LIST OF THE THINGS YOU DO IN YOUR PRESENT DAY TO DAY LIFE
AND THEN MAKE A LIST OF THE THINGS YOU WILL BE DOING IN YOUR LIFE WITH YOUR DEFINITION OF SUCCESS ACHIEVED.
ONCE YOU DO SO, BEGIN TO TAKE ACTION IN ADJUSTING YOUR LIFE ACCORDINGLY WITHIN EACH MOMENT.

SUBCONSCIOUS LIMITING BELIEFS ARE THE BELIEFS YOU HAVE ABSORBED OR CREATED
THROUGHOUT YOUR LIFETIME THAT LIMIT YOU FROM ACHIEVING YOUR PERSONAL DEFINITION OF SUCCESS.

IT IS VERY IMPORTANT THAT YOU ARE GENTLE WITH YOURSELF WHEN DISCOVERING AND TRANSFORMING
EACH OF YOUR SUBCONSCIOUS LIMITING BELIEFS.

RECOGNIZE THAT YOUR SUBCONSCIOUS LIMITING BELIEFS ARE THE STORY YOU LIVE BY DAY TO DAY WITHIN YOUR MIND, AND THAT THEY EXTERNALIZE INTO YOUR WAKING REALITY. THEY HAVE (AND CONTINUE TO) SHAPE YOUR REALITY AS YOU KNOW IT BECAUSE THEY ARE THE SOURCE FROM WHICH YOU PULL YOUR REACTIONS, YOUR IDEAS AND OVERALL HOW YOU INTERACT WITH ANYONE OR ANYTHING IN LIFE. EACH INDIVIDUAL HAS A SUBCONSCIOUS MIND AND THE MAJORITY OF THAT SUBCONSCIOUS MIND TAKES FORM IN THE EARLY YEARS OF LIFE (YEARS 0-7). DURING THIS TIME THE SUBCONSCIOUS MIND ABSORBS ALL INFORMATION AND TEACHINGS AS TRUE. THE SOURCES OF THIS INFORMATION VARY WITHIN EACH INDIVIDUAL, BUT THE MOST COMMON SOURCES ARE: PARENTS, THE PEOPLE WHO RAISED YOU, THE PEOPLE WHO INFLUENCED YOU, PAST EXPERIENCES, AND WHICHEVER CULTURE/SOCIETY YOU ARE BORN INTO. ALL OF THE SOURCES ALSO HAVE SUBCONSCIOUS MINDS, THOSE SUBCONSCIOUS MINDS HAVE ALSO BEEN SHAPED BY OTHERS WHO CAME BEFORE THEM, IT IS NOT THEIR FAULT FOR TEACHING YOU THE LIMITING BELIEFS. IF YOU HAVE CHILDREN: BE MINDFUL & AWARE OF WHAT YOU ARE PLACING AS TRUTH WITHIN THEIR SUBCONSCIOUS MINDS, BLESS THEM EARLY ON WITH EMPOWERING BELIEFS. AS ADULTS WE MUST UNCOVER WHAT OUR SUBCONSCIOUS BELIEFS ARE, DECIDE WHETHER THEY SUPPORT OUR DEFINITION OF SUCCESS AND DESIRED LIFE DESIGN, THEN RETRAIN OUR SUBCONSCIOUS MIND TO EMBODY THE TRUTH WE HAVE DECIDED UPON FOR OURSELF - TRANSFORMING THE LIMITING BELIEFS THAT HAVE PREVIOUSLY HINDERED OUR SUCCESS AND CREATING A BEAUTIFUL, EMPOWERING SUBCONSCIOUS BELIEF SYSTEM THAT COMPLETELY SUPPORTS OUR DESIRED LIFE DESIGN. YOU ARE AN ETERNAL BEING AND DESERVE TO HAVE A SUBCONSCIOUS MIND FILLED WITH NOTHING BUT EMPOWERING BELIEFS!

THE NEXT PAGE SERVES AS A GUIDE FOR DISCOVERING YOUR OWN SUBCONSCIOUS LIMITING BELIEFS, AND HOW TO TRANSFORM THEM INTO SUBCONSCIOUS EMPOWERING BELIEFS!

YOU ARE PURE LOVE AT YOUR CORE,
AN INFINITE BEING THAT HAS BEEN COVERED IN SKIN AND GIFTED THIS HUMAN LIFETIME -
TO DREAM AND CREATE A BLISSFUL AND FULFILLING LIFE BEYOND YOUR WILDEST DREAMS.

YOU ARE A MIRACLE IN THE FLESH, DO NOT EVER FEEL THAT YOU ARE ANYTHING LESS.

CREATING SUBCONSCIOUS EMPOWERING BELIEFS

RECREATING YOUR SUBCONSCIOUS BELIEF SYSTEM TO WORK FOR YOU & NOT AGAINST YOU!

WHEN YOUR CONSCIOUS MIND IS FOCUSED ON YOUR DESIRED MANIFESTATIONS
BUT YOUR SUBCONSCIOUS LIMITING BELIEFS ARE GEARED TOWARDS BELIEVING THE EXACT OPPOSITE
YOU WILL FEEL LIKE YOU ARE CONSTANTLY FACING THE INABILITY TO MANIFEST THE THINGS YOU DESIRE.
(AND THE LIFE YOU DESIRE!)
THAT IS WHY IT IS CRUCIAL TO IDENTIFY THEM AND RECREATE THEM
SO THAT THEY WILL NOW WORK FOR YOU AND THEY WILL NO LONGER BE AGAINST YOU.

I WILL MAKE THIS SIMPLE, LET'S BEGIN!

FIRST, RECOGNIZE THAT (MOST LIKELY)
YOU ARE NOT CONSCIOUSLY AWARE OF ALL YOUR SUBCONSCIOUS LIMITING BELIEFS.
THEY ARE DEEP INSIDE YOU AND MUST BE EXTRACTED OUT BY **YOU** THROUGH FOLLOWING THE PROCESS BELOW.
ALSO RECOGNIZE THAT **THIS IS A PROCESS AND TAKES TIME.**
AND THINGS MAY CONTINUE TO SURFACE AT LATER TIMES.
SO **BE GENTLE WITH YOURSELF**.

FOCUS ON WORKING WITH ONE AT A TIME.
KNOW THAT YOU DO NOT NEED TO 'PERFECT' YOUR SUBCONSCIOUS IN ORDER TO MANIFEST YOUR DESIRES ~
IMPROVE WHILE YOU MANIFEST ~ IMPROVING & MANIFESTING GO HAND IN HAND.

[REFER TO THE MIND & MANIFESTATION WARM UP PAGE]
CLOSE YOUR EYES FOR A FEW MINUTES, CONNECT WITH YOUR HEARTBEAT, BREATH AND INNER POWER.

TAKE OUT YOUR JOURNAL AND ASK YOURSELF: WHAT ARE MY LIMITING BELIEFS IN REGARDS TO ___.
CORE AREAS INCLUDE: HEALTH, LOVE, WEALTH, RELATIONSHIPS, MONEY.
(WRITE DOWN ANYTHING AND EVERYTHING THAT COMES TO MIND. THIS IS NOT A TIME FOR JUDGEMENT
OR PERFECTION, WRITE ALL YOUR INNERMOST BELIEFS DOWN IN YOUR JOURNAL.)

ALL OF YOUR LIMITING BELIEFS ARE NOW LISTED OUT.

TO CREATE AN EMPOWERING SUBCONSCIOUS BELIEF SYSTEM
WRITE DOWN EXACT OPPOSITE OF EACH LIMITING BELIEF YOU HAVE IDENTIFIED.
MODIFY EACH BELIEF INTO THE EXACT FORM YOUR BELIEFS WOULD BE IN
WHILE LIVING A LIFE FAR BEYOND WHAT YOU COULD EVER DREAM OF OR IMAGINE.
THIS WILL SEEM SO **UNNATURAL** AND **STRANGE** SINCE THEY ARE NOT YOUR TRUTH NOW,
BUT DEEP DOWN THEY REALLY DO **FEEL** PLEASURABLE TO YOU PERSONALLY ..
AND YOU REALLY DO WISH THEY WERE YOUR REALITY.
REMEMBER, SINCE YOU ARE LITERALLY GOING AGAINST THE TRUTH
THAT IS **ENGRAINED SO DEEPLY** INTO YOUR MIND--IT WILL FEEL STRANGE. THAT IS OK, THAT MEANS THIS IS
WORKING! ONCE YOU HAVE YOUR LIST OF EMPOWERING BELIEFS WRITE EACH OF THEM INTO A PRESENT TENSE
STATEMENT. WRITE THESE STATEMENTS IN A PLACE WHERE YOU CAN EASILY REFLECT ON THEM, AND DO SO OFTEN.
THE MORE YOU DO SO THE MORE **NATURAL** THEY WILL BEGIN TO **FEEL** AND THE MORE YOUR SUBCONSCIOUS MIND
WILL BEGIN TO ACCEPT THEM AS **TRUTH**, AND SUPPORT YOUR DESIRES AND DESIRED LIFE DESIGN. A GREAT TIME TO
REFLECT ON THESE PRESENT TENSE STATEMENTS IS IN THE MORNING
WHILE YOU ARE JUST WAKING UP FROM YOUR SLEEP AND RIGHT BEFORE YOU GO TO BED.
RIGHT BEFORE BED YOU ARE ABOUT TO SINK INTO YOUR SUBCONSCIOUS MIND
WHERE YOU WILL BE **MARINATING** FOR THE NEXT 8 HOURS (GIVE OR TAKE). THE STATE OF MIND YOU ARE IN
5-10 MINUTES BEFORE FALLING ASLEEP, AND ALL THE WAY INTO FALLING ASLEEP,
SETS THE TONE FOR THE VIBRATIONAL FREQUENCY IN WHICH YOU ARE DREAMING--
THE VIBRATIONAL FREQUENCY YOU ARE TRAINING YOUR SUBCONSCIOUS MIND TO ACCEPT AS **TRUTH,**
THUS YOUR SUBCONSCIOUS WILL SUPPORT THE MANIFESTATION OF THIS VIBRATION WITHIN YOUR LIFE.
WHAT EXACTLY DO YOU WANT YOUR SUBCONSCIOUS MIND TO HELP YOU MANIFEST WITHIN YOUR LIFE?
DURING YOUR WAKING HOURS START TAKING THE INSPIRED ACTION STEPS TOWARDS YOUR DESIRES -
DO THE THINGS THAT TRULY SCARE YOU THE MOST.
THE REASON THESE THINGS SCARE YOU IS BECAUSE YOUR LIMITING BELIEF SYSTEM IS SCREAMING:
NO THAT IS AGAINST WHAT I KNOW AS TRUE! STOP! PLEASE, STAY WHERE IT IS SAFE AND COMFORTABLE!
AND YOU ARE ACTIVELY TRANSFORMING YOUR LIMITING BELIEFS INTO EMPOWERING BELIEFS BY REVOLTING!
YOU ARE NOW CHASING DOWN THE THINGS THAT SCARE YOU THE MOST,
TAMING THEM AND TRAINING THEM TO WORK WITH YOU AND FOR YOU!

FINANCIAL MANIFESTATIONS

KNOW WHAT YOU WILL DO WITH YOUR INCREASE IN FINANCES.
MAKE A LIST OF WHAT YOU DESIRE,
& WHAT YOU WILL BE USING YOUR MONEY FOR.

HAVING CLARITY IS CRUCIAL.
KNOW THE DETAILS IN REGARDS TO WHAT YOU ARE DESIRING & ASKING THE UNIVERSE FOR.

WITH X AMOUNT OF MONEY I WILL (FILL IN THE BLANK).

MAKE A LIST

OUR BELIEFS AROUND FINANCES ARE SOMETHING WE HAVE BUILT BASED UPON
THE BELIEFS OF THE PEOPLE WHO HAVE BEEN AROUND US OUR ENTIRE LIFE.
WE CAN CHANGE OUR FINANCIAL SITUATION BY CHANGING OUR FINANCIAL MINDSET & BELIEF SYSTEM.

JOURNAL EVERYTHING YOU DESIRE.
THERE IS NO JUDGEMENT,
WE HAVE INFINITE ABUNDANCE AVAILABLE TO US ALL,
FINANCIAL ABUNDANCE IS A VIBRATIONAL FREQUENCY THAT MUST BE MATCHED INTERNALLY
BEFORE IT IS SEEN AS MANIFESTED EXTERNALLY WITHIN OUR PHYSICAL REALITY.

I AM ALIGNED WITH THE ENERGETIC FREQUENCY OF ABUNDANCE.

THE UNIVERSE DOES NOT GIVE YOU A DREAM THAT MATCHES YOUR BUDGET.
THE UNIVERSE IS NOT CHECKING YOUR BANK ACCOUNT, THE UNIVERSE IS CHECKING
THE LEVEL OF FAITH & CERTAINTY YOU HOLD IN REGARDS TO IT'S ABILITY TO SUPPORT
AND NURTURE YOU. IT ALWAYS MATCHES YOUR ENERGY FREQUENCY, YOU CANNOT LIE
TO THE UNIVERSE WHEN IT COMES TO YOUR FREQUENCY YOU ARE EMITTING
EVERYTHING IS EXPOSED & REFLECTED BACK TO YOU.
EMBODY & EXPERIENCE THE FEELINGS OF FAITH OVER FEAR IN EVERY MOMENT.

I ELIMINATE PROCRASTINATION & FEAR
WITH ACTION & LOVE.

Goddess Life Designer

MY SUBCONSCIOUS ONLY LISTENS TO
MY HIGHER SELF

PHYSICAL BODY / HEALTH MANIFESTATIONS

I AM NOT MY BODY. IN MY PUREST FORM I AM DIVINELY PERFECT, I AM AN ETERNAL BEING.

WHILE HERE ON EARTH I HAVE A HUMAN BODY,
AND WITH THAT BODY I AM ABLE TO DO MANY AMAZING THINGS.

I DECIDE HOW I LOVE MY BODY. I
DECIDE WHAT MAKES ME FEEL MY BEST IN REGARDS TO MY PHYSICAL APPEARANCE.

A SIMPLE FORMULA FOR ANY DESIRED PHYSICAL BODY CHANGES AND/OR HEALTH CHANGES:

BE CLEAR ON THE PHYSICAL CHANGES / HEALTH CHANGES THAT YOU DESIRE. WRITE THEM OUT.

CREATE PRESENT TENSE STATEMENTS FOR THESE CHANGES.
TRAIN YOURSELF TO KNOW THAT THIS IS NOW YOUR REALITY,
EVEN BEFORE ANY CHANGES HAVE OCCURRED.
VISUALIZE YOURSELF WITH THOSE CHANGES AS REALITY.
EMBODY THE CHANGES WITHIN EVERY FIBER OF YOUR BEING.
THE CHANGES YOU DESIRE ARE YOURS.

CREATE A PLACEBO FOR THE CHANGES YOU DESIRE. DO RESEARCH, BUT DO NOT OBSESS OVER THE METHOD
YOU ARE WORKING WITH. JUST BELIEVE THAT DOING (FILL IN THE BLANK WITH YOUR PLACEBO) WILL
CREATE THE CHANGE YOU DESIRE. DOING THIS IN COMBINATION WITH TRAINING YOUR SUBCONSCIOUS
MIND THROUGH REVIEWING YOUR PRESENT TENSE STATEMENTS AND EMBODYING THE CHANGES AS
ALREADY PRESENT WILL CREATE THE CHANGES YOU DESIRE.

DO NOT COUNTER YOUR PROCESS WITH DOUBTS OR NEGATIVITY..
THIS WILL BLOCK YOUR DESIRED CHANGES.
YOU MUST FULLY BELIEVE AND EMBODY THESE CHANGES AS HERE NOW, EVEN BEFORE THEY ARE PRESENT.

Manifesting Love

WE ARE PURE LOVE AT OUR CORE, AND THAT IS WHY LOVE IS THE GREATEST EMOTION WE CAN FEEL AS HUMAN BEINGS. EVERYONE'S DEFINITION OF LOVE WILL BE DIFFERENT, AND THAT IS PERFECT. THERE IS NO MOLD FOR WHAT LOVE MUST MEAN TO ALL OF US. WE GET TO DEFINE OUR TRUEST DEFINITION OF THE WORD FOR OUR OWN SELF AND BE THE EMBODIMENT OF THAT WITHIN OUR OWN LIFE. HOW BEAUTIFUL.

THERE ARE MANY FORMS OF LOVE EXISTING WITHIN OUR WORLD.
ALWAYS KNOW THAT YOU ARE ENTIRELY WHOLE ON YOUR OWN.
BE SURE THAT YOU CAN FIRST LOVE YOURSELF ENTIRELY BEFORE ATTEMPTING TO LOVE ANOTHER.
ALSO BE SURE THAT YOUR POTENTIAL 'LOVER' CAN LOVE THEIR OWN SELF ENTIRELY BEFORE ATTEMPTING TO LOVE YOU. KNOW THAT YOU DO NOT HAVE TO HAVE A ROMANTIC PARTNER TO BE HAPPY, FIND YOUR DEFINITION OF LOVE, EMBODY THAT & ATTRACT A LIFE FILLED WITH THAT DEFINITION OF LOVE.

WHEN IT COMES TO MANIFESTING A ROMANTIC PARTNER WE OFTEN TIMES HAVE OUR EYES AND HEART SET ON A SPECIFIC PERSON. WRITE DOWN ALL OF THE QUALITIES YOU BELIEVE THIS SPECIFIC PERSON HAS (THE REASONS WHY YOU ARE ATTRACTED TO THEM AND DESIRE THEM). IF YOU DON'T HAVE A SPECIFIC PERSON IN MIND THEN WRITE DOWN ALL THE QUALITIES YOU WOULD LOVE TO HAVE IN A ROMANTIC PARTNER. INCLUDE: PHYSICAL QUALITIES, MENTAL QUALITIES, SPIRITUAL QUALITIES, ETC. EVEN INCLUDE THE THINGS THAT YOU WILL DO TOGETHER AND THE BOUNDARIES THAT YOU AGREE ON WITHIN YOUR RELATIONSHIP. LIST ALL OF THE THINGS THAT ARE IMPORTANT TO YOU. FEEL AMAZING WHILE YOU ARE DOING THIS, REALLY GET INTO YOUR MOST PURE LOVE STATE. ONCE YOU HAVE FINISHED WRITING - CLOSE YOUR EYES AND IMAGINE THIS PERSON - ONLY NOW, BLUR OUT THIS PERSON'S FACE AND NAME IN YOUR MIND - THIS IS IMPORTANT TO DO BECAUSE THE PERSON YOU THINK YOU WANT MAY NOT ACTUALLY BE THE PERSON YOU BELIEVE THEY ARE, AND THERE IS A PERSON OUT THERE WITH THOSE EXACT QUALITIES YOU DESIRE YOUR PARTNER TO HAVE - SO, DO NOT LIMIT YOURSELF! USE THE BLUR TECHNIQUE. FOR A FEW MINUTES THINK ON HOW AMAZING YOUR ROMANTIC RELATIONSHIP WITH THIS PERSON FEELS. THEN, THANK THE UNIVERSE FOR SENDING YOU THIS PERSON, OR SOMEONE EVEN MORE PERFECT FOR YOU! LET GO AND KNOW THAT THE UNIVERSE IS BRINGING YOU THIS PERSON IN THE MOST PEACEFUL AND LOVING WAY. THERE IS NO NEED TO WONDER WHERE THEY ARE OR WHEN THEY WILL APPEAR. JUST CONTINUE TO FEEL GOOD EACH DAY BY DOING THE THINGS YOU LOVE, THE THINGS THAT MAKE YOU FEEL YOUR BEST. EMBODY THE PERSON THAT YOU WILL BE IN THIS RELATIONSHIP RIGHT NOW AND THROUGHOUT EACH MOMENT OF YOUR DAY. MAKE THIS FUN. FEEL THAT YOU ARE IN LOVE. DO NOT WAIT FOR THE RELATIONSHIP TO ARRIVE IN ORDER TO BEGIN EMBODYING THE WAY YOU WILL THINK, ACT, FEEL, DRESS, BEHAVE AND CARRY YOURSELF IN YOUR ROMANTIC RELATIONSHIP. DO IT ALL NOW, BE THAT PERSON NOW.

IF YOU ALREADY HAVE A ROMANTIC PARTNER [THIS ALSO APPLIES TO ANY RELATIONSHIP, NOT JUST ROMANTIC] AND WANT TO MANIFEST MORE LOVE WITHIN YOUR RELATIONSHIP DO SO BY GETTING REALLY CLEAR ON WHAT LOVE MEANS TO YOU, AND WHAT MAKES YOU FEEL LOVED THE MOST. FOCUS ON WHAT YOU LOVE THE MOST ABOUT THIS PERSON AND TELL THEM, EXPRESS YOUR LOVE TO THIS PERSON IN THE UNIQUE WAYS THAT MAKES THEM FEEL THE MOST LOVED. STUDY THEM, GET TO KNOW THEM BETTER. BY SHOWING THEM THAT YOU APPRECIATE AND LOVE THEM IT WILL BEGIN TO BE REFLECTED BACK TO YOU FROM THEM. DO NOT GO ABOUT THIS EXPECTING THEM TO SHOW YOU MORE LOVE, BUT RATHER BE THE LOVE THAT YOU DESIRE TO RECEIVE. TELL THEM ALL THE AMAZING THINGS YOU LOVE AND APPRECIATE ABOUT THEM.

GRATITUDE WORKS MIRACLES IN ALL AREAS OF LIFE - LOVE IS NO EXCEPTION.

Goddess Life Designer

ASK FOR SIGNS FROM THE UNIVERSE & BELIEVE YOU WILL RECEIVE THEM.

ASK FOR SIGNS SPECIFIC TO YOURSELF TO BE PLACED IN YOUR LIFE & MADE OBVIOUS TO YOU THAT THEY ARE YOUR SIGNS.

ALWAYS HANDWRITE EACH OF YOUR GOALS/DESIRES IN THE PRESENT TENSE, & GIVE THANKS IN ADVANCE, AS THOUGH THEY HAVE ALREADY COME TRUE. THIS TRAINS YOUR SUBCONSCIOUS MIND TO ACCEPT IT AS YOUR TRUTH & FURTHER SUPPORT YOU. EVERYTHING WILL **FEEL** MORE NATURAL& EFFORTLESSLY ALIGN.

FEEL IT VIBRATING IN EVERY FIBER OF YOUR BEING AS ALREADY HERE. MEDITATE ON THIS, YOU MUST KNOW WHAT IT WILL FEEL LIKE TO HAVE YOUR GOAL MANIFEST AS TRUTH IN THE PHYSICAL PLANE. IGNITE ALL 6 SENSES, IN NO PARTICULAR ORDER. JUST FOCUS ON THE TRUE FEELINGS WITH EACH SENSE & ALIGN EFFORTLESSLY WITH INSPIRED FLOW.

1. WHAT IS YOUR OVERALL INTUITIVE VIBE WHILE EXPERINCING THIS GOAL FULFILLED?

2. SEE
3. HEAR
4. SMELL
5. TASTE
6. TOUCH

MEDITATE ON THE FEELINGS OF ALL 6 SENSES IN THE FEELING OF YOUR GOAL REACHED & FULFILLED. [[AT LEAST ONCE A DAY]]

BE IN A CONSTANT MINDSET OF GRATITUDE & MIRACLES

YOUR END GOAL IS DETERMINED BY YOU, WITH CRYSTAL CLEAR DEFINITION & CERTAINTY, THE UNIVERSE PROVIDES THE 'HOW', & AS YOU MOVE FORWARDS WITH ALL THE STEPS PROVIDED YOU ARE BECOMING A MASTER OF LIFE MAPPING AND DESIGNING YOU WILL RECEIVE UNEXPECTED GUIDANCE, INSPIRATION & MIRACLES.

ALIGN YOURSELF & IMMERSE YOURSELF

WITHIN THE IMMENSITY OF ABUNDANCE THE UNIVERSE HAS TO OFFER

MORE THAN EVER. REMIND YOURSELF, HOWEVER YOU CAN, TO REMAIN

IN THE MOMENT & CERTAIN OF YOURSELF. FEEL THE POTENCY OF YOUR

ETERNAL GODDESS POWER EMANATING THROUGHOUT

EVERY SINGLE FIBER OF YOUR EXISTENCE.

Just Breathe, Goddess, you've got this!

PLACE THE TIP OF YOUR TONGUE
ON THE ROOF OF YOUR MOUTH,
RIGHT BEHIND YOUR FRONT TEETH.
BREATH IN THROUGH NOSE FOR THE COUNT OF 4.
HOLD FOR THE COUNT OF 7.
SLOWLY RELEASE YOUR BREATH FROM MOUTH FOR THE COUNT OF 8.

[ALSO WORKS WONDERS WHEN YOU ARE HAVING TROUBLE FALLING ASLEEP.]

RATHER THAN BECOMING STRESSED OR ANXIOUS
ABOUT ANYTHING OR ANY SITUATION THAT WILL TAKE PLACE IN THE FUTURE
WRITE DOWN YOUR ABSOLUTE IDEAL OUTCOME FOR THE GIVEN SITUATION.
GET TO KNOW & FEEL THAT AS YOUR TRUTH.
FEEL THAT, FOR CERTAIN, THIS WILL BE YOUR OUTCOME.

LEAVE NO ROOM FOR DOUBT. THIS IS JUST AS ANY OTHER DESIRE/GOAL.

KNOW & FEEL
THAT EVERYTHING IS TAKEN CARE OF
JUST HOW YOU MANIFESTED IT.

KNOW THYSELF:
KNOW WHAT MAKES YOU FEEL YOUR BEST
& TURN TO THESE ACTS OF SELF LOVE.
[REFLECT ON THE SELF LOVE PAGE]

YOUR WORD IS YOUR WAND.
EVERY INTENTION BEHIND EACH WORD YOU HAVE
WRITTEN, THOUGHT OR SPOKEN IS COMING BACK AS
THE EXACT SAME VIBE YOU SENT IT OUT AS.

THIS CREATIVE MAGIC WITHIN YOU CAN NOT BE TURNED OFF,
IT IS SIMPLY ABOUT WHETHER OR NOT YOU WANT TO ACKNOWLEDGE &
HARNESS IT FOR YOUR BEST INTEREST & PERSONAL DESIRES.
PRODUCING YOUR TRUEST BLISS & INFINITE ABUNDANCE.

THE ENERGY OF EACH ATMOSPHERE OR SITUATION IS DETERMINED BY
OUR EMOTIONAL ENERGY WE ARE EACH RADIATING.

YOU DON'T NEED TO FEEL ANY OTHER WAY BESIDES BLISSFUL.
YOU CHOOSE YOUR REALITY,
THERE IS ALWAYS A DIFFERENT THOUGHT & FEELING TO CHOOSE.
THE UNIVERSE CREATES THE PATH TO THE OUTCOME YOU
EMBODY WITH CERTAINTY.
IF YOU ARE FEELING LIKE SHIT & EXPECTING THE WORST,
THE UNIVERSE THINKS THAT IS WHAT YOU ARE ASKING FOR MORE OF.
THE UNIVERSE LISTENS TO YOUR FEELINGS.
IT CREATES FOR YOU EXACTLY WHAT YOU ARE ASKING FOR.
THIS IS WHY EMBODYING THE FEELING OF YOUR DESIRE(S) AS AN ALREADY
ESTABLISHED REALITY IS SO POTENT IN
THE SUCCESSFUL MANIFESTATION OF YOUR DESIRED LIFE DESIGN.

IF YOU ARE DISTRESSED BY ANYTHING EXTERNAL, THE PAIN IS
NOT DUE TO THE THING ITSELF, BUT TO YOUR ESTIMATE OF IT;
AND THIS YOU HAVE THE POWER TO REVOKE AT ANY MOMENT.
-MARCUS AURELIUS

I VIEW ANY REJECTION OR PERCEIVED LOSS AS A PUSH FROM THE
UNIVERSE TO VIBRATE EVEN HIGHER & DREAM EVEN BIGGER..

BEING TRUE TO OURSELVES IS ALWAYS FIRST PRIORITY.
ALLOWING OURSELVES TO ACCEPT THAT WE FEEL NEGATIVITY
IS MUCH BETTER THAN FIGHTING AGAINST IT.
THE PERMITTING OF OUR EMOTIONS IS AN ACT OF SELF LOVE.
RATHER THAN BEING FALSELY OPTIMISTIC WE ARE ACCEPTING, PROCESSING AND
TRANSFORMING OUR EMOTIONS
IN ORDER TO STAY ALIGNED WITH OUR HIGHEST PURPOSE,
IMMERSING DEEPER INTO OUR PASSIONS & BLISS.
ALLOWING OURSELVES TO BE OUR OWN TRUTH.

Goddess Life Designer

I SURRENDER CONTROL

Surrender is a loving bliss you owe to your soul~

IN HER BOOK, 'CREATING YOUR HEART'S DESIRE',
SONIA CHOQUETTE TALKS ABOUT HAVING AN ALCHEMY BOX.
I LOVE HER WORK. I HAVE ALSO HEARD MANY OTHERS SPEAK OF RITUALS FOR LETTING GO.
SO, BELOW IS A GENERAL EXAMPLE FOR AN ALCHEMY VESSEL/SPACE.

YOUR MIND DOES NOT EVER REALLY WANT TO SURRENDER CONTROL,
UNLESS YOU ACTUALLY DO SOMETHING THAT LETS YOUR KNOW
YOU ARE NO LONGER IN CONTROL.

UNTIL YOU DO THAT RITUAL, YOUR MIND IS GOING TO KEEP GOING BACK TO IT.

YOU HAVE TO DO A RITUAL, BECAUSE THAT IS HOW THE MIND LEARNS TO SURRENDER CONTROL.

THE RITUAL OF CREATING A VESSEL, WHICH CAN BE A BOX, OR ANYTHING YOU CHOOSE.
A TRIANGLE IS USED AS IN THE JOHN OF GOD COMMUNITY TO REPRESENT FAITH, LOVE AND CHARITY.

IT DOESN'T HAVE TO BE A VESSEL, EITHER.
IT COULD ALSO BE A SACRED PLACE [BIG OR SMALL] OF YOUR OWN.

ANCIENT CIVILIZATIONS WOULD PRAY AS A COLLECTIVE GROUP,
AND IF ANY ONE OF THE INDIVIDUALS WOULD HAVE SOME KIND OF SPECIAL REQUEST
THEY WOULD TAKE IT TO THE TEMPLE AND THEY WOULD LEAVE IT.
SOMETIMES THEY WOULD PUT IT IN A SPECIAL VESSEL, PRAY OVER IT, AND THEN LEAVE IT.
DOING THAT TOLD THEM THEY WERE PUTTING IT IN THE HANDS OF THE UNIVERSE.

YOU CAN DO THAT TOO, BY CREATING A SPECIAL VESSEL OR PLACE
[OR COMBINATION OF BOTH], WHERE YOU PLACE YOUR SURRENDERED REQUESTS.

WHEN YOU ARE AT THE PLACE WHERE YOU HAVE DONE YOUR WORK AND YOU ARE READY TO REST
YOU CAN USE YOUR OWN ALCHEMY VESSEL/SPACE IN RITUAL.

AN ALCHEMY VESSEL IS DECORATED BY YOU,
TO BE MEANINGFUL & SACRED,
WHATEVER THAT ENTAILS FOR YOU PERSONALLY.
BE PLAYFUL & LOVE THE PROCESS OF CREATING YOUR ALCHEMY VESSEL.

RITUAL

WRITE DOWN WHAT YOU WANT & SURRENDER IT TO YOUR VESSEL.

AFTER A FEW DAYS OF MEDITATING ON YOUR COMPLETE SURRENDER BURN YOUR REQUEST. [SAFELY]
THIS IS TO SHOW THAT YOU HAVE FULLY SURRENDERED THE REST OF THE WORK TO THE UNIVERSE.

GO ABOUT YOUR DAILY LIFE IN A HIGH VIBRATIONAL MINDSET -- A GRATEFUL MINDSET.
THINK ON WHAT MAKES YOU FEEL GOOD NOW.
WHAT ARE YOU GRATEFUL FOR?
FEEL AMAZING WHILE ALLOWING THE UNIVERSE TO TAKE OVER.
MATCH THE RADIANT FREQUENCY OF YOUR DESIRE FULFILLED.

THE DETAILS & QUESTIONS TO INSPIRE SUCCESS
OF EACH GOAL YOU SET USING S.M.A.R.T.:

S
I PROVIDE ABSOLUTE CLARITY ON THE DETAILS FOR WHAT IT IS I DESIRE.
THIS KEEPS ME FOCUSED & MOTIVATED,
THE UNIVERSE RESPONDS BEST TO SPECIFIC DETAILS,
IT WANTS TO GIVE US OUR DESIRES--SO WE MUST KNOW THE DETAILS OF WHAT WE WANT IN
ORDER TO HAVE THAT MANIFESTED AS OUR REALITY.

ANSWER THESE 5 QUESTIONS:
(1) WHAT DO I WANT TO ACCOMPLISH?
(2) WHY IS THIS IMPORTANT?
(3) WHO IS INVOLVED?
(4) WHERE IS IT LOCATED?
(5) ARE THERE RESOURCES/LIMITS?

M
MY GOAL MAKES ME FEEL MOTIVATED TO TAKE ACTION.
IS MEANINGFUL TO MY DESIRED LIFE DESIGN,
AS WELL AS
MEASURABLE IN TERMS OF TRACKING PROGRESSION.

ANSWER THESE 3 QUESTIONS:
(1) HOW MUCH?
(2) HOW MANY?
(3) HOW WILL I KNOW WHEN I CAN SAY I HAVE ACCOMPLISHED MY GOAL?

A
MY GOAL IS ATTAINABLE.

(1) THIS CAN BE DETERMINED BY ASSESSING MY PERSONAL BELIEF SYSTEM,
& ASKING MYSELF WHAT I BELIEVE I AM TRULY CAPABLE OF ACHIEVING.
I BELIEVE I AM CAPABLE OF ACHIEVING _____ ALONGSIDE THE UNIVERSES FULL SUPPORT,
THE UNIVERSE IS WORKING WITH ME & FOR ME,
BECAUSE WHEN I MOVE THE UNIVERSE MOVES WITH ME.
THE UNIVERSE AND & I ARE A POWERFUL COMBO.
I AM GRATEFUL MY FAITH IS EVER EXPANDING BECAUSE I ALWAYS SEE THE BEST RESULTS WHEN
I BELIEVE WITH EVERY FIBER OF MY BEING.
(2) ALSO, DO I HAVE ACCESS TO THE RESOURCES I NEED
IN ORDER TO BE ACTIONABLE TOWARDS MY GOAL AT THIS TIME?

R
I HAVE DETERMINED HOW MUCH MY GOAL MATTERS TO ME.
I AM CERTAIN THIS GOAL RESONATES WITH MY DESIRES FOR MY LIFE DESIGN.

I AM ABLE TO ANSWER YES TO THESE QUESTIONS:
(1) DOES THIS SEEM WORTHWHILE?
(2) IS THIS THE RIGHT TIME?
(3) DOES THIS ALIGN WITH MY OTHER EFFORTS/NEEDS?

T
MY GOAL IS TIME SENSITIVE
& MOVING ME TOWARDS THE LIFE DESIGN I DESIRE.

DETERMINING QUESTIONS:
(1) WHEN WILL I REACH MY GOAL?
(2) WHAT CAN I COMPLETE BY SPECIFIC DATES?
(3) WHAT CAN I DO TODAY TO MOVE ME TOWARDS ACHIEVING MY GOAL?

SIMPLY WRITING YOUR GOALS ON PAPER MAKES YOU MUCH MORE LIKELY TO ACHIEVE THEM.

BLUEPRINT FOR MANIFESTING LONG TERM GOALS

REFLECT ON THE JOURNALING YOU HAVE DONE SO FAR,
THEN JOURNAL ALONGSIDE FOLLOWING PROMPTS:

WHERE WOULD YOU ABSOLUTELY LOVE TO SEE YOURSELF IN 5 YEARS?
THINK ABOUT THIS IN A PLAYFUL STATE OF MIND..
REMEMBER, THIS IS YOUR LIFE & YOU CAN EDIT IT AS FREQUENTLY AS YOU DESIRE TO!

ONE YEAR GOAL:
ONE YEAR GOALS ARE MEANT FOR DREAMING BIG!
KEEP THIS GOAL IN ALIGNMENT WITH WHERE YOU WOULD LOVE TO SEE YOURSELF IN 5 YEARS.

WHAT IS YOUR 3 MONTH GOAL?
IS IT IN ALIGNMENT WITH YOUR ONE YEAR GOAL?

WHAT IS YOUR 6 MONTH GOAL?
IS IT IN ALIGNMENT WITH YOUR ONE YEAR GOAL?

WHAT IS YOUR 9 MONTH GOAL?
IS IT IN ALIGNMENT WITH YOUR ONE YEAR GOAL?

Goddess Life Designer

ALIGN
EACH MOON CYCLE
ACCORDINGLY
WITH YOUR ONE YEAR GOAL.
USE THE 3, 6 & 9 MONTH GOALS AS
BULLET POINTS,
DUE DATES,
& AN ALIGNMENT TOOL
FOR YOUR ONE YEAR GOAL.
MAKING SURE YOU ARE KEEPING YOUR MOON CYCLE GOALS
A
L
I
G
N
E
D
EACH CYCLE IS CRUCIAL.

START WITH YOUR ONE YEAR GOAL, THEN YOUR 3, 6 & 9 MONTH GOALS AS A BREAKDOWN OF YOUR ONE YEAR GOAL. THEN, REFLECT ON THESE GOALS AS YOU COMPOSE YOUR NEW MOON DESIRES FOR EACH INDIVIDUAL CYCLE.

THIS EXAMPLE IS FOR ONE YEAR GOALS, BUT APPLIES TO ALL GOALS YOU WILL BE SETTING

Today is: (date one year from today),

 it is: (specific time of your choosing),

and I am/have: (description of goal/desire achieved),

I know this because:*   *Goddess Life Designer*

*(following the description of your goal/desire achieved make sure to ignite and write about all of your senses for what you are feeling in THIS moment you are writing about, & reiterate what you have accomplished to get you to this place of fulfillment & success. Your inspired actions & accomplishments PLUS the universe EQUALS your goal/desire manifested into reality.)

EXAMPLE:

Today is April 22, 2019 (date one year from today), it is 8:13 p.m. (specific time chosen), and I am relaxing by the fireplace in my beautiful stone and brick home I have purchased this year, it is in the most ideal and beautiful location I could ever dream of (description of goal/desire achieved). I feel so warm inside because I am always being reminded of how infinitely supported I am by the universe. Sitting here right now is an example of how I know this. My desires have been fulfilled into my reality and my intuitive vibes are always guiding me towards the highest good in every moment. I am thankful for my life, I am grateful that I am able to inspire and move so many beautiful souls into their own most blissful and fulfilling life design. I see the flames inside the fireplace dancing around as I enjoy this moment of reflection and warmth. I smell the burning wood fragrances filling my home. I taste the tea I am sipping and forever after it will remind me of this moment. I am so comfortable in this moment. The inside of my heart is reflecting what is outside. My body wrapped in these plush blankets and soft clothes, my heart is overflowing with gratitude, generosity, and love. It is in these moments of relaxation, reflection and gratitude that I feel the most inspiration and love.

1. WHAT IS YOUR OVERALL INTUITIVE VIBE WHILE EXPERINCING THIS GOAL FULFILLED?

2. WHAT DO YOU SEE
3. HEAR
4. SMELL
5. TASTE
6. TOUCH

USE THIS SAME DESIGN FOR YOUR MONTHLY LUNAR GOALS, AND YOUR 3, 6 & 9 MONTH GOALS. SIMPLY CHANGE THE DATES & TIMES. THEN, ADD INFORMATION ACCORDINGLY

DO NOT GET CONSUMED WITH THE 'HOW.' THIS IS THE UNIVERSE'S PART TO HANDLE. JUST HAVE FAITH, AND MOVE. WHEN YOU MOVE, THE UNIVERSE MOVES WITH YOU.

THE JOURNEY IS THE DESTINATION.
-DAN ELDON

THE SOLAR YEAR
IS WILLING TO BE UNIQUELY DESIGNED BY YOU, GODDESS.
TAKING FORM ONE COMPLETED MOON CYCLE AFTER THE OTHER,
TO ULTIMATELY REACH YOUR
ONE YEAR [SOLAR] GOAL
BE SURE TO REFER TO THE DAILY JOURNALING PROMPTS EVERY SINGLE DAY
-THEY ARE IN THE BACK OF THE GODDESS LIFE DESIGNER- FOR EASY ACCESS.

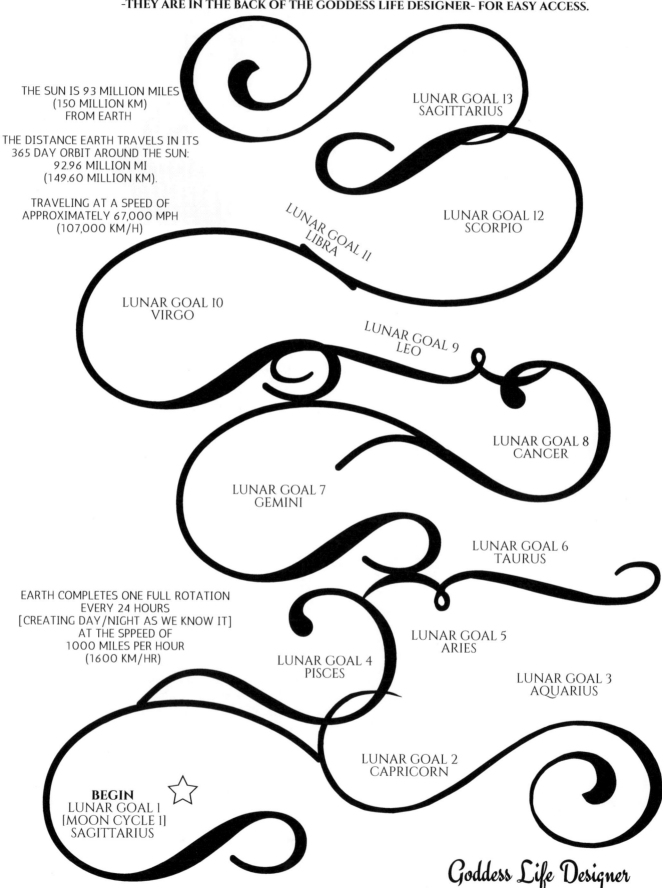

THE SUN IS 93 MILLION MILES
(150 MILLION KM)
FROM EARTH

THE DISTANCE EARTH TRAVELS IN ITS
365 DAY ORBIT AROUND THE SUN:
92.96 MILLION MI
(149.60 MILLION KM).

TRAVELING AT A SPEED OF
APPROXIMATELY 67,000 MPH
(107,000 KM/H)

EARTH COMPLETES ONE FULL ROTATION
EVERY 24 HOURS
[CREATING DAY/NIGHT AS WE KNOW IT]
AT THE SPPEED OF
1000 MILES PER HOUR
(1600 KM/HR)

LUNAR GOAL 13
SAGITTARIUS

LUNAR GOAL 12
SCORPIO

LUNAR GOAL 11
LIBRA

LUNAR GOAL 10
VIRGO

LUNAR GOAL 9
LEO

LUNAR GOAL 8
CANCER

LUNAR GOAL 7
GEMINI

LUNAR GOAL 6
TAURUS

LUNAR GOAL 5
ARIES

LUNAR GOAL 4
PISCES

LUNAR GOAL 3
AQUARIUS

LUNAR GOAL 2
CAPRICORN

BEGIN
LUNAR GOAL 1
[MOON CYCLE 1]
SAGITTARIUS

Goddess Life Designer

MOON PHASES DEFINED

Each of the moon phases has been given a page for reflection,
meditation & journaling.
Use these pages as a tool
during the appropriate times of each moon cycle
to harness, align & **AMPLIFY**
your creative manifestation powers.

Goddess Life Designer

Create your own rituals that resonate with each lunar phase & cycle.

Ignite more passion & inspirational flow.

An example:

Align yourself through prayer & meditation.
Journal as you feel pleasurable,
Create an I am affirmation for the outcome you desire
from this cycle/phase.
Write it down on paper.
Surrender this paper to your sacred vessel or space.
Once your surrender has sunk into every fiber of your being
burn the paper [safely].
Feel yourself surrender even more to the divine, infinitely abundant
universe which is existing within & outside of your being.

[[add various elements as you please to ignite all your senses]]

NEW MOON

Goddess Life Designer

I NOW MEDITATE ON WHAT GOAL/DESIRE I WILL BE MANIFESTING THIS MOON CYCLE.
I AM PLANTING THE SEED I DESIRE TO MANIFEST.

MY FIRST ACTION IS REFERRING BACK TO THE MIND & MANIFESTATION WARM UP PAGE.

THEN, I REFLECT ON ALL OF THE INSPIRATIONAL PAGES OF THE GODDESS LIFE DESIGNER.

I PAY SPECIAL ATTENTION TO, AND SPEND MORE TIME ON THE S.M.A.R.T. GOAL SETTING

PAGE. I JOURNAL THE QUESTIONS THIS PAGE PROMPTS ME TO

IN REGARDS TO THE DESIRE I AM CHOOSING TO MANIFEST THIS MOON CYCLE.

I DO THIS FOR INSPIRATION, ALIGNMENT, STRUCTURE & CRYSTAL CLARITY

IN THE DETAILS OF THE DESIRE I HAVE DECIDED UPON.

ONCE I HAVE DECIDED WHAT MY DESIRE FOR THIS LUNAR MONTH IS, USING S.M.A.R.T., I REFER TO THE GOAL SCRIPTING FORMULA PAGE TO SCRIPT MY NEW MOON INTENTION FOR THIS LUNAR CYCLE.

KEEP IN MIND: FOR THE "TODAY IS: ____" PORTION OF THE SCRIPT YOU WILL USE
THE LAST DAY OF THE CURRENT MOON CYCLE,
WHICH IS THE LAST DAY OF THE BALSAMIC MOON PHASE FOR ANY GIVEN MOON CYCLE.

FOR EXAMPLE: THE LAST DAY OF THE BALSAMIC MOON PHASE IS JAN. 15, 2018 FOR THE FIRST MOON CYCLE, AND FEB. 14, 2018 FOR THE SECOND MOON CYCLE.

THE SPECIFIC PAGE FOR EACH CYCLE PROVIDES DATES FOR EACH PHASE.

MY INSPIRED ACTIONS & ACCOMPLISHMENTS THIS CYCLE PLUS THE UNIVERSE EQUALS MY GOAL/DESIRE MANIFESTED INTO REALITY.

I AM ACTIVELY SETTING MY GOAL/DESIRE THROUGHOUT THIS PHASE.

WHEN I HAVE COMPLETED MY WRITTEN FORMAT OF MY GOAL,
I SPEAK IT OUT LOUD TO MYSELF.
I REVISE IT AS I PLEASE, SO THAT IT FEELS RIGHT WITHIN ME.

I INVITE MY DESIRE INTO MY LIFE, THROUGH FEELING IT AS MY PRESENT REALITY.

DISPLAY A WRITTEN COPY OF THIS MOON CYCLE'S DESIRE SOMEWHERE SIGNIFICANT TO YOU SO THAT YOU ARE REGULARLY VIEWING IT ~ IN ORDER TO ~ FEEL THE HIGH VIBRATIONS OF GRATITUDE FOR ITS PHYSICAL MANIFESTATION WITHIN YOUR LIFE.

CRESCENT MOON

Goddess Life Designer

I TRULY TAKE TIME TO RELAX & JOURNAL MY FEELINGS
ON WHAT MY DESIRE FEELS LIKE AS ALREADY MANIFESTED IN MY LIFE.

I ALLOW MYSELF TO DAY DREAM ON THIS MOMENT IN TIME.

I FEEL MY INNER GODDESS POWER IN CONNECTION WITH THE DIVINE.

I REMIND MYSELF TO TAKE A FEW MOMENTS OUT OF MY DAY HERE AND
THERE, JUST TO OBSERVE ALL MY SENSES & BREATHE.

I SPEND TIME MEDITATING ON DETAILS OF WHAT MY DESIRE FEELS LIKE AS ALREADY MANIFESTED.

I CLEANSE MY LIFE OF ANY TOXIC RELATIONSHIPS, OLD CLUTTER & WORK SITUATIONS

THAT NO LONGER BENEFIT MY LIFE DESIGN.

I REFLECT ON THE POWER IN CLEAN & TIDY PAGE

AND ANY OTHER PAGES I AM RESONATING WITH AT THIS TIME.

WORDS OF WISDOM FROM DR. WAYNE DYER:

WHEN YOU CARRY AROUND RESENTMENT INSIDE OF YOU ABOUT ANYTHING OR ANYONE IT

WILL END UP HARMING YOU AND CREATING IN YOU A SENSE OF DESPAIR.

NO ONE EVER DIES FROM A SNAKE BITE; THE VENOM THAT CONTINUES TO POUR THROUGH

YOUR SYSTEM AFTER THE BITE IS WHAT WILL DESTROY YOU.

I MAKE SURE MY ENTIRE BEING IS CLEANSED OF ALL THAT IS NOT SERVING MY
HIGHEST GOOD & DESIRED LIFE DESIGN.
MY MIND BECOMES RELAXED, FOCUSED & CLEAR.
NOW MY DESIRE HAS THE ATTENTION & SPACE TO MANIFEST AS REAL.

**I AM IN A SELF LOVE PHASE,
I ALLOW MYSELF TO RELAX & REENERGIZE.
I AM TREATED WITH LOVE & RESPECT.**

FIRST QUARTER MOON

Goddess Life Designer

I TAKE ACTION TOWARD MY GOAL/DESIRE.
I ALLOW MYSELF TO BE FLEXIBLE & OPEN-MINDED IN REGARDS TO MY DESIRE.
DOING SO ALLOWS ME TO BE OPEN TO RECEIVING SOMETHING EVEN BETTER.

I ALLOW POSITIVITY TO FLOW INTO THE SPACE I CREATED WITHIN
THE PAST FEW DAYS OF CLEANSING ALL THAT WAS NO LONGER
SERVING MY HIGHEST GOOD & DESIRED LIFE DESIGN.

I AM INSPIRED
& MOVE WITH AN EMBODIMENT OF DEDICATED ACTION TOWARDS MY GOAL/DESIRE.

I BREATHE IN INSPIRING ENERGY FROM MY DIVINE LIFE SOURCE,
I PAUSE & FEEL THE INFINITE ABUNDANCE AVAILABLE TO ME,
I EMANATE OUT MY BEING MY PUREST FORMS OF CREATIVE MAGIC.

AS I GROW I KNOW THAT MY POWER IS NOT IN EXTERNAL OBJECTS,
MY POWER IS WITHIN MY OWN SELF. I AM MY POWER.
MY POWER: THE SAME REASON I AM ALIVE IN THIS MOMENT,
THE SAME ETERNAL POWER FUELING MY EXISTENCE.

AN EXAMPLE OF HOW I DO FIND PEACE IN ENJOYING CERTAIN OBECTS,
FOR THEY HOLD A PERSONAL SYMBOLISM TRUE TO MYSELF:
MY AMETHYST THAT FITS PERFECTLY INTO THE PALM OF MY CLOSED HAND,
SERVING AS A REMINDER TO ME, OF MY INTERNAL POWER.
& MY DREAM CATCHERS,
I APPRECIATE THEIR BEAUTY IN REMINDING ME I AM ALWAYS DESIGNING THIS DREAM.

I FEEL MY GOAL AS ALREADY MANIFESTED INTO MY REALITY.

GIBBOUS MOON

Goddess Life Designer

I TAKE TIME TO RELAX & TRUST THAT THE UNIVERSE HAS MY BACK.
EVERYTHING IS BEING ALIGNED IN DIVINE, PERFECT TIME.

THIS IS AN AMAZING TIME FOR A RITUAL OF SURRENDER.

I MEDITATE ON MY DESIRES & I ADD MORE DETAIL INTO WHAT THEY FEEL LIKE
AS ALREADY MANIFESTED INTO MY LIFE.

I BRING IN MORE SENSES & VITALITY, I BRING MY DREAMS TO LIFE.

I TAKE THE TIME TO FEEL 'AS IF' MY DESIRES HAVE BEEN FULFILLED.
HOW WILL I CARRY MYSELF NOW?
HOW WILL I DRESS, LOOK & BEHAVE NOW?
HOW WILL I SPEND MY TIME?
HOW **EXACTLY** HAS THIS CHANGED MY LIFE?
WHAT IS MY OVERALL VIBE IN EXPERIENCING THE TRUE FULFILLMENT OF MY DESIRES?
HOW DOES THIS REALLY **FEEL** HAVING THE
MANIFESTED FORM OF MY DESIRE EMANATING THROUGHOUT
EVERY SINGLE FIBER OF MY EXISTENCE?
HOW APPRECIATIVE AM I FEELING?!?

I WRITE A PRESENT TENSE JOURNAL SCRIPT FOR A DAY IN LIFE 'AS IF'
MY DESIRES HAVE ALREADY BEEN FULFILLED.
THIS HELPS ME TO GET IN FLOW WITH THE AMAZING FEELINGS
OF THE PLEASURABLE DETAILS OF MY MANIFESTATION FULFILLED.
I FEEL MY DESIRE WITH **CLARITY**,
I AM VERY FAMILIAR WITH THE FEELINGS ITS FULFILLED FORM BRINGS.
I AM ALWAYS FREE TO EDIT MY DESIRE ~
I AM NOT BONDED BY MY 'ORIGINAL' DESIRE.
I AM THE CREATOR OF MY REALITY & BEING FLEXIBLE ALLOWS ME TO ALWAYS BE OPEN TO
WELCOMING A LIFE BEYOND MY WILDEST DREAMS.

**I AM IN A SELF LOVE PHASE, I ALLOW MYSELF TO RELAX & REENERGIZE.
I TREAT MYSELF GENTLY.**

I ALLOW MYSELF TO RELEASE THE URGE TO CONTROL,
I FOLLOW MY VISION WITH A BLISSFUL, PLAYFUL VIBRANCY
IN THE HEART OF MY BEING.
I REFLECT ON THE 'I SURRENDER CONTROL' PAGE.

I GIVE THANKS IN ADVANCE FOR MY DESIRES MANIFESTED.
**I SURRENDER TO A POWER GREATER THAN MYSELF,
CREATING SPACE FOR LOVING BLISS TO FILL & INSPIRE MY BEING.**

FULL MOON

Goddess Life Designer

**I CONTINUE TAKING DAILY INSPIRED ACTION TOWARDS MY GOAL/DESIRE.
I AM FEELING 'FULL' OF FAITH & INSIGHT AT THIS TIME.**

I ILLUMINATE ALONGSIDE THE MOON,
I CAN SEE WITH CLARITY,
THE WISDOM I ALREADY HOLD WITHIN ME.
EVERYTHING IS ALREADY WITHIN ME.

I AM BLOSSOMING FROM WITHIN.

I AM FULFILLING MY DREAMS BY DESIGNING & TAKING INSPIRED ACTION TOWARDS MY DREAMS.

I SURRENDER & RELEASE FOR CLEANSING
ANY HOLDS FOR CONTROL I HAVE IN REGARDS TO MY DESIRES.
I RELEASE THEM TO THE GREATEST WILL OF THE DIVINE SOURCE OF MY BEING, AS
I TRUST I AM BEING GUIDED & SUPPORTED IN EACH MOMENT.

I MOVE FORWARD WITH SUPPORTIVE ACTION TOWARDS MY GOAL/DESIRE.

I REFLECT ON MY JOURNALING I HAVE DONE SO FAR THIS MOON CYCLE.
I CONTINUE TO MEDITATE & DAYDREAM ON THE FEELINGS AND
EACH OF MY SENSES AS THOUGH MY DESIRES ARE COMPLETELY FULFILLED.

I ALLOW MYSELF TO DAY DREAM.
I ALLOW MYSELF TO ACT ON INSPIRATION.
I ALLOW MYSELF TO LOVE & BE LOVE.
I AM DESIGNING THE LIFE I DESIRE THROUGH MY OWN PASSION & BLISS.
MY DIVINE LIFE SOURCE IS ALWAYS FULLY SUPPORTING ME.

DISSEMINATING MOON

Goddess Life Designer

I RELAX & GIVE GENUINE THANKS AS MY DESIRE BEGINS MANIFESTING INTO TRUE FORM.

I REFLECT INTO MY OWN SELF & UNCOVER ANY LIMITING BELIEFS
I MAY HAVE LINGERING DEEP INSIDE OF ME.

I ASSES ANY DOUBTS THAT I FEEL TOWARDS MY SUCCESS & MANIFESTATION CAPABILITIES.
I REFLECT ON THE SUBCONSCIOUS LIMITING BELIEFS PAGE.

I PERFORM A RITUAL OF RELEASE FOR SELF-LIMITING BELIEFS & BRING IN CONFIDENCE,
LOVE & KNOWINGNESS OF THE UNIVERSES SUPPORT TOWARDS ME.
I REFLECT ON THE I SURRENDER CONTROL PAGE.

I AM IN A SELF LOVE PHASE, I ALLOW MYSELF TO RELAX & REENERGIZE.

I MEDITATE ON MY LIFE'S PURPOSE NOW.
I REFLECT ON THE JOURNALING I HAVE DONE IN REGARDS TO MY PASSIONS
& DESIRES. I EDIT MY LIFE DESIGN AS I PLEASE.
I GIVE THANKS FOR THE GUIDANCE I RECEIVE NOW,
ALLOWING ME TO EVOLVE TO MY TRUEST,
MOST FULFILLING POTENTIAL IN THIS LIFE.

I AM GRATEFUL THAT EVERYTHING IS IN ALIGNMENT WITH THE
HIGHEST GOOD FOR ALL.

I CONTINUE TO FEEL MY DESIRE AS MANIFESTED IN MY LIFE.

THIRD QUARTER MOON

Goddess Life Designer

**I ACTIVELY MEDITATE ON & SPEAK OUTLOUD MY I AM AFFIRMATIONS.
I REFLECT ON THE I AM AFFIRMATIONS PAGE**

AM I MINDFUL IN BEING OPEN TO RECEIVING SIGNS FROM THE UNIVERSE?

AM I HOLDING ON TO MY DESIRED OUTCOME TOO TIGHT??

DOING SO WILL RESTRICT MY DESIRES FROM FLOWING INTO MY LIFE,
I MUST TRUST THAT EVERYTHING I DESIRE IS COMING TO ME
IN THE MOST PEACEFUL AND LOVING WAY.
IT IS CRUCIAL THAT I CREATE THE SPACE FOR MY DESIRES TO ENTER INTO MY LIFE.
IF I AM ALWAYS OBSESSING OVER THE OUTCOME ..
I AM NOT TRULY LETTING GO AND ALLOWING THE UNIVERSE TO DO ITS PART.
THE ART OF SURRENDER IS ABSOLUTELY CRUCIAL WITHIN MANIFESTATION.
IT FEELS AMAZING TO LET GO AND ALLOW.
IT IS EASIER TO LET GO THAN TO TRY TO CONTROL ALL THE LITTLE DETAILS,
AND CONSTANTLY WONDER WHERE MY DESIRE IS.
I LET GO AND I KEEP MY VIBRATIONS HIGH BY DOING THINGS I LOVE
& BY KEEPING THE VIBRATIONAL FREQUENCY OF MY THOUGHTS SO VERY HIGH!!
THIS ALLOWS MY ENERGETIC FREQUENCY TO MATCH
THE FULFILLMENT OF MY DESIRED OUTCOME
-NOT THE FEELINGS OF LACK OR 'WELL, WHERE IS IT?'

I NOW JOURNAL & REFLECT ON MY OWN PERSONAL BELIEFS, LIFE VALUES & BOUNDARIES.
I TAKE THE TIME TO DO SO IN REGARDS TO EVERY SINGLE AREA OF MY LIFE.
KEEPING A WRITTEN COPY OF MY PERSONAL BELIEFS & BOUNDARIES IS A WONDERFUL TOOL,
ALLOWING ME TO CONSISTENTLY BE IN ALIGNMENT WITH MY DESIRED LIFE DESIGN.
CREATING BOUNDARIES MAY NOT ALWAYS BE EASY BUT IT IS NECESSARY,
AND OVER TIME I DO REALIZE HOW VERY EMPOWERING IT IS!
REMEMBER THIS:
THE ONLY PEOPLE WHO WILL EVER BE UPSET BY YOU SETTING BOUNDARIES ARE
THE ONES THAT BENEFITTED FROM YOU HAVING NONE.

**JOURNALING THROUGH THIS LIFE DESIGNER KEEPS ME GROWING
EVER-INCREASINGLY STRONGER. IT IS AN ACT OF SELF LOVE.**

BALSAMIC MOON

Goddess Life Designer

I AM GRATEFUL FOR ALL THAT I HAVE ACHIEVED
& RECEIVED THIS MOON CYCLE.

I AM IN A SELF LOVE PHASE, I ALLOW MYSELF TO RELAX & REENERGIZE.

I AM BEING GENTLE & AT PEACE WITH MYSELF IN THE LAST MOON PHASE,

AS I LET GO OF ALL THAT DOES NOT SERVE ME.

I EMBODY AN EVER-INCREASING FAITH IN MY OWN GROWTH.

I CELEBRATE ALL OF MY ACCOMPLISHMENTS, BOTH BIG AND SMALL.

BY RESTING & TAKING PART IN SELF LOVE RITUALS I PREPARE TO TAKE ACTION AGAIN.

I NOW LET GO OF ANYTHING I AM TRYING TOO HARD TO CONTROL

WITHIN MY OWN LIFE.

I RECOGNIZE I MUST LET GO OF OBSESSING OVER

DETAILS & THE HOWS.

IN DOING SO I ALLOW THE UNIVERSE FREEDOM & SPACE TO MOVE WITH ME

IN WAYS MUCH GREATER THAN I COULD EVER PREDICT OR CONTROL.

I AM FEELING PHENOMENAL & INSPIRED AS I RELAX DEEPER INTO MY
APPRECIATION, CONFIDENCE, SUCCESS, INFINITE LOVE
& ALIGNMENT WITH THE UNIVERSE.

I ALLOW MYSELF TO SINK INTO MY PASSIONS & FAITH IN THE UNIVERSE.

THE SPECIFIC MOON CYCLES

ONE MOON CYCLE, FROM NEW MOON TO NEW MOON, LASTS 29-30 DAYS.

[ON AVERAGE] THE MOON IS 238,855 MILES (384,400 KM) FROM EARTH.

THE MOON TRAVELS AT 2,288 MPH (3,683 KM PER HOUR) AROUND THE EARTH.

DURING THIS TIME IT TRAVELS A DISTANCE OF 1,423,000 MILES (2,290,000 KM).

THE MOON TRAVELS AROUND THE EARTH 13 TIMES IN ONE YEAR.

Goddess Life Designer

EACH MOON CYCLE
OF 2018
HAS ITS OWN PAGE.
AN OVERVIEW FOR
WHAT WE WILL BE WORKING WITH DURING
THAT PARTICULAR CYCLE,
& A REFERENCE TOOL FOR
THE DATES OF EACH PHASE OF THAT CYCLE.
USE THE MOON CYCLE PAGES ALONG WITH
THE MOON PHASE PAGES
WHEN CREATING YOUR DESIRE SCRIPT
FOR EACH NEW MOON.

THESE PAGES ARE PROVIDED TO KEEP YOU ALIGNED WITH
THE MOON CYCLES & PHASES OF 2018.
PROVIDING AN INSPIRATIONAL OVERVIEW FOR
[BUT NOT IN-DEPTH DESCRIPTIONS OF]
THE ASTROLOGICAL INSIGHTS FOR EACH INDIVIDUAL CYCLE.
I HIGHLY RECOMMEND MYSTICMAMA.COM FOR WELL EXPLAINED, IN-DEPTH
INSIGHTS AND INSPIRATION DURING EACH NEW AND FULL MOON.
IMMERSE YOURSELF IN WISDOM FROM THE SOURCES YOU DESIRE ~

MOON CYCLE
GOAL

LUNAR
ALIGNMENT

New Moon in **Sagittarius**

Areas of focus under the Sagittarius New Moon:

We now uncover how we can express the characteristic energies
of the archer within our desired life design:

Meditate on these affirmations and then journal what you feel being
brought to attention within your own being. After journaling, create
your New Moon Design script for the Sagittarius New Moon.

I am defining my life passions & desires blissfully, exactly as I desire.
_____ is what sparks my curiosity.
_____ is what living a meaningful life means to me.
I am nurturing my faith & surrendering my urges to control
any & all outcomes, big or small.
I am connected to the right people, places & experiences in every moment,
I trust that.
My truth exposed & illuminated with bliss feels like this:

Beginning on the New Moon Dec. 17-19, 2017

Crescent moon dates: Dec. 20-24, 2017

First quarter moon dates: Dec. 25-27, 2017

Gibbous moon dates: Dec. 28-31, 2017

Full moon dates: Jan. 1-4, 2018

Full [wolf] moon in Cancer, sun in Capricorn (opposite of Cancer)

Disseminating moon dates: Jan. 5-7, 2018

Third quarter moon dates: Jan. 8-11, 2018

Finishing with the Balsamic Moon Jan. 12-15, 2018

MOON CYCLE
GOAL

LUNAR
ALIGNMENT

NEW MOON IN **CAPRICORN**

AREAS OF FOCUS UNDER THE CAPRICORN NEW MOON:

WE NOW UNCOVER HOW WE CAN EXPRESS THE CHARACTERISTIC ENERGIES
OF THE GOAT WITHIN OUR DESIRED LIFE DESIGN:

MEDITATE ON THESE AFFIRMATIONS AND THEN JOURNAL WHAT YOU FEEL BEING
BROUGHT TO ATTENTION WITHIN YOUR OWN BEING. AFTER JOURNALING, CREATE
YOUR NEW MOON DESIGN SCRIPT FOR THE CAPRICORN NEW MOON.

MY DETERMINATION TO SUCCEED IS FUELED BY:
I AM AMBITIOUS IN PURSUING MY PASSIONS & DESIRES.
I AM DEDICATED BECAUSE:
_____ KEEPS ME MOTIVATED:

BEGINNING ON THE NEW MOON JAN. 16-19, 2018

CRESCENT MOON DATES: JAN. 20-23, 2018

FIRST QUARTER MOON DATES: JAN. 24-27, 2018

GIBBOUS MOON DATES: JAN. 28-30, 2018

FULL MOON DATES: JAN. 31-FEB. 2, 2018
FULL [BLUE] MOON IN LEO, SUN IN AQUARIUS (OPPOSITE OF LEO)

'BLUE MOON' REFERS TO THE SECOND FULL MOON WITHIN THE SAME MONTH.
[TOTAL LUNAR ECLIPSE JAN. 31.]

DISSEMINATING MOON DATES: FEB. 3-6, 2018

THIRD QUARTER MOON DATES: FEB. 7-10, 2018

FINISHING WITH THE BALSAMIC MOON FEB. 11-14, 2018

MOON CYCLE
GOAL

LUNAR
ALIGNMENT

New Moon in **Aquarius**

Areas of focus under the Aquarius New Moon:

We now uncover how we can express the characteristic energies
of the water bearer within our desired life design:

Meditate on these affirmations and then journal what you feel being brought to
attention within your own being. After journaling, create your new moon design
script for the Aquarius New Moon.

This is how I can make things better within my life:
To be the change I want to see in the world would require that I:
Being my most authentic soul consists of:
My life is full of pure bliss & enjoyment because every day consists of me doing:

Beginning on the New Moon Feb. 15-18, 2018

CRESCENT MOON DATES: FEB. 19-22, 2018

FIRST QUARTER MOON DATES: FEB. 23-25, 2018

GIBBOUS MOON DATES: FEB. 26-28, 2018

FULL MOON DATES: MARCH 1-4, 2018

Full [worm] moon in Virgo , sun in Pisces (opposite of Virgo)

DISSEMINATING MOON DATES: MARCH 5-8, 2018

THIRD QUARTER MOON DATES: MARCH 9-12, 2018

Finishing with the Balsamic Moon : March 13-16, 2018

MOON CYCLE
GOAL

LUNAR
ALIGNMENT

New Moon in **Pisces**

Areas of focus under the Pisces New Moon:

We now uncover how we can express the characteristic energies
of the two fish within our desired life design:

Meditate on these affirmations and then journal what you feel being brought to
attention within your own being. After journaling, create your new moon design
script for the Pisces New Moon..

I contain an abundance of love.
This is what true love looks like to me:
I am loving to myself in these specific ways:
These are ways I can be more self loving:
I am always strengthening my connection with my inner divine Goddess,
to radiate pure love & life.

Beginning on the New Moon March 17-19, 2018

Crescent Moon Dates: March 20-23, 2018

First Quarter Moon Dates: March 24-26, 2018

Gibbous Moon Dates: March 27-30, 2018

Full Moon Dates: March 31- April 2, 2018

Full [blue] moon in Libra , sun in Aries (opposite of Libra)

Disseminating Moon Dates: April 3-7, 2018

Third Quarter Moon Dates: April 8-11, 2018

Finishing with the Balsamic Moon : April 12-14, 2018

MOON CYCLE
GOAL

LUNAR
ALIGNMENT
New Moon in **Aries**

Areas of focus under the Aries New Moon:

We now uncover how we can express the characteristic energies
of the ram within our desired life design:

This is the sign you've been waiting for: your fresh start is here now.
Be open to receiving new, blissful opportunities.
Cheers to new beginnings!

Meditate on these affirmations and then journal what you feel being brought
to attention within your own being. After journaling, create your new moon
design script for the Aries New Moon..

I am fearless in defining & acting upon what I desire.
I lead my life in the direction of my choosing because I am worthy.
This is what I can do to elevate my bravery:
I am abundantly receiving as result of the fulfillment of my innermost desires.

Beginning on the New Moon April 15-18, 2018

CRESCENT MOON DATES: APRIL 19-21, 2018

FIRST QUARTER MOON DATES: APRIL 22-25, 2018

GIBBOUS MOON DATES: APRIL 26-28, 2018

FULL MOON DATES: APRIL 29- MAY 2, 2018

Full [pink] moon in Scorpio, sun in Taurus (opposite of Scorpio)

DISSEMINATING MOON DATES: MAY 3-6, 2018

THIRD QUARTER MOON DATES: MAY 7-10, 2018

Finishing with the Balsamic Moon : May 11-14, 2018

MOON CYCLE
GOAL

LUNAR
ALIGNMENT

NEW MOON IN **TAURUS**

AREAS OF FOCUS UNDER THE TAURUS NEW MOON:

WE NOW UNCOVER HOW WE CAN EXPRESS THE CHARACTERISTIC ENERGIES
OF THE BULL WITHIN OUR DESIRED LIFE DESIGN:

MEDITATE ON THESE AFFIRMATIONS AND THEN JOURNAL WHAT YOU FEEL BEING BROUGHT TO ATTENTION
WITHIN YOUR OWN BEING.
AFTER JOURNALING, CREATE YOUR NEW MOON DESIGN SCRIPT FOR THE TAURUS NEW MOON..

I ALLOW MYSELF TO RELAX AND BE REWARDED.
THIS IS HOW I CAN RELAX, IN ORDER TO CREATE OPTIMAL SPACE
& ALIGNMENT FOR MONEY TO FLOW ABUNDANTLY INTO MY LIFE:

I CAN ___ TO COMFORT, PLEASE & SOOTHE MY UNIQUE SOUL ..
DOING SO ALLOWS ME TO SINK DEEPER IN TUNE WITH MY FEELING BASED SENSES.
GETTING ME OUT OF MY HEAD & INTO MY BODY.

I APPRECIATE EARTH, AS SHE IS [ALSO] A LIVE AND FLOURISHING GODDESS.
I EAT WHOLE FOOD FROM HER, I PLANT LIFE INTO HER.

BEGINNING ON THE NEW MOON MAY 15-17, 2018

CRESCENT MOON DATES: MAY 18-20, 2018

FIRST QUARTER MOON DATES: MAY 21-24, 2018

GIBBOUS MOON DATES: MAY 25-28, 2018

FULL MOON DATES: MAY 29- JUNE 1, 2018

FULL [FLOWER] MOON IN SAGITTARIUS, SUN IN GEMINI (OPPOSITE OF SAGITTARIUS)

DISSEMINATING MOON DATES: JUNE 2-5, 2018

THIRD QUARTER MOON DATES: JUNE 6-9, 2018

FINISHING WITH THE BALSAMIC MOON : JUNE 10-12, 2018

MOON CYCLE
GOAL

LUNAR
ALIGNMENT

NEW MOON IN **GEMINI**

AREAS OF FOCUS UNDER THE GEMINI NEW MOON:

WE NOW UNCOVER HOW WE CAN EXPRESS THE CHARACTERISTIC ENERGIES
OF THE TWINS WITHIN OUR DESIRED LIFE DESIGN:

MEDITATE ON THESE AFFIRMATIONS AND THEN JOURNAL WHAT YOU FEEL BEING BROUGHT
TO ATTENTION WITHIN YOUR OWN BEING. AFTER JOURNALING, CREATE YOUR
NEW MOON DESIGN SCRIPT FOR THE GEMINI NEW MOON..

I HAVE THE MOST FUN WHEN I AM:
I AM ABLE TO CREATE MORE PLAYFULNESS IN MY LIFE BY:
I LOVE TO ENGAGE MY MIND IN THESE SPECIFIC WAYS:
I AM COMMUNICATING WELL, IN SUPPORT OF MY DESIRES.

BEGINNING ON THE NEW MOON JUNE 13-15, 2018

CRESCENT MOON DATES: JUNE 16-19, 2018

FIRST QUARTER MOON DATES: JUNE 20-22, 2018

GIBBOUS MOON DATES: JUNE 23-26, 2018

FULL MOON DATES: JUNE 27- JULY 1, 2018

FULL [ROSE] MOON IN CAPRICORN, SUN IN CANCER (OPPOSITE OF CAPRICORN)

DISSEMINATING MOON DATES: JULY 2-5, 2018

THIRD QUARTER MOON DATES: JULY 6-8, 2018

FINISHING WITH THE BALSAMIC MOON : JULY 9-11, 2018

MOON CYCLE
GOAL

LUNAR
ALIGNMENT

New Moon in **Cancer**

Areas of focus under the Cancer New Moon:

We now uncover how we can express the characteristic energies of the crab within our desired life design:

Meditate on these affirmations and then journal what you feel being brought to attention within your own being. After journaling, create your new moon design script for the Cancer New Moon..

I am able to bring more peace into my life by:
I am able to bring more feelings of safety & security into my life by:
I am in love with my home.
I have a sacred space of my own.

Beginning on the New Moon July 12-15, 2018

Crescent Moon Dates: July 16-18, 2018

First Quarter Moon Dates: July 19-22, 2018

Gibbous Moon Dates: July 23-26, 2018

Full Moon Dates: July 27-30, 2018

Full [thunder] moon in Aquarius, sun in Leo (opposite of Aquarius)

Disseminating Moon Dates: July 31- Aug. 3, 2018

Third Quarter Moon Dates: Aug. 4-6, 2018

Finishing with the Balsamic Moon : Aug. 7-10, 2018

MOON CYCLE
GOAL

LUNAR
ALIGNMENT

New Moon in Leo

Areas of focus under the Leo New Moon:

We now uncover how we can express the characteristic energies
of the lion within our desired life design:

Meditate on these affirmations and then journal what you feel being brought to
attention within your own being. After journaling, create your
new moon design script for the Leo New Moon..

I am constantly finding ways to express my creativity,
my favorite ways are:

My ambition drives me to take the roads less traveled,
I am confident I will always be divinely supported.

I am attracting the love I desire to receive,
by embodying those attributes within myself first, they are:

Beginning on the New Moon Aug. 11-13, 2018

CRESCENT MOON DATES: AUG. 14-17, 2018

FIRST QUARTER MOON DATES: AUG. 18-21, 2018

GIBBOUS MOON DATES: AUG. 22-25, 2018

FULL MOON DATES: AUG. 26-29, 2018

Full [sturgeon] moon in Pisces, sun in Virgo (opposite of Pisces)

DISSEMINATING MOON DATES: AUG. 30- SEPT. 1, 2018

THIRD QUARTER MOON DATES: SEPT. 2-5, 2018

Finishing with the Balsamic Moon : Sept. 6-8, 2018

MOON CYCLE
GOAL

LUNAR
ALIGNMENT

New Moon in **Virgo**

Areas of focus under the Virgo New Moon:

We now uncover how we can express the characteristic energies
of the virgin within our desired life design:

Meditate on these affirmations and then journal what you feel being brought to
attention within your own being. After journaling, create your
new moon design script for the Virgo New Moon..

I am always desiring for the highest good of all humanity.
I am physically well,
I love my body because:
To show more love to my body I can:
I am financially stable and that feels amazing because:
I am balanced within all aspects of my life.

Beginning on the New Moon Sept. 9-11, 2018

CRESCENT MOON DATES: SEPT. 12-15, 2018

FIRST QUARTER MOON DATES: SEPT. 16-19, 2018

GIBBOUS MOON DATES: SEPT. 20-23, 2018

FULL MOON DATES: SEPT. 24-27, 2018

Full [harvest] moon in Aries, sun in Libra (opposite of Aries)

DISSEMINATING MOON DATES: SEPT. 28- OCT. 1, 2018

THIRD QUARTER MOON DATES: OCT. 2-4, 2018

Finishing with the Balsamic Moon : Oct. 5-7, 2018

MOON CYCLE
GOAL

LUNAR
ALIGNMENT

New Moon in **Libra**

Areas of focus under the Libra New Moon:

We now uncover how we can express the characteristic energies
of the scales within our desired life design:

Meditate on these affirmations and then journal what you feel being brought
to attention within your own being. After journaling, create your new moon
design script for the Libra New Moon..

I am emanating fairness, peace & harmony within my life in these specific ways:
I am strengthening my support systems
& my faith in the universe supporting me at all moments.
I give thanks for all supportive relationships in my life.
I meditate on all yin & yang aspects of my being
by journaling what comes to me when I think of each within myself.
I give thanks.

Beginning on the New Moon Oct. 8-11, 2018

CRESCENT MOON DATES: OCT. 12-15, 2018

FIRST QUARTER MOON DATES: OCT. 16-19, 2018

GIBBOUS MOON DATES: OCT. 20-23, 2018

FULL MOON DATES: OCT. 24-26, 2018

Full [hunter's] moon in Taurus, sun in Scorpio (opposite of Taurus)

DISSEMINATING MOON DATES: OCT. 27-30, 2018

THIRD QUARTER MOON DATES: OCT. 31- NOV. 2, 2018

Finishing with the Balsamic Moon : Nov. 3-6, 2018

MOON CYCLE
GOAL

LUNAR
ALIGNMENT

New Moon in **Scorpio**

Areas of focus under the Scorpio New Moon:

We now uncover how we can express the characteristic energies
of the scorpion within our desired life design:

Meditate on these affirmations and then journal what you feel being brought
to attention within your own being. After journaling,
create your new moon design script for the Scorpion New Moon..

I am in control of my destiny.
The intense passion & desire I feel within bring me motivation
& determination in these ways:
My actions inspired through motivation & determination bring the most
fulfilling forms of wealth & abundance into my life.
This is Intimacy defined by me:

Beginning on the New Moon Nov. 7-10, 2018

CRESCENT MOON DATES: NOV. 11-14, 2018

FIRST QUARTER MOON DATES: NOV. 15-18, 2018

GIBBOUS MOON DATES: NOV. 19-21, 2018

FULL MOON DATES: NOV. 22-25, 2018

Full [frost] moon in Gemini, sun in Sagittarius (opposite of Gemini)

DISSEMINATING MOON DATES: NOV. 26-28, 2018

THIRD QUARTER MOON DATES: NOV. 29- DEC. 2, 2018

Finishing with the Balsamic Moon : Dec. 3-5, 2018

MOON CYCLE
GOAL

LUNAR
ALIGNMENT

New Moon in **Sagittarius**

Areas of focus under the Sagittarius New Moon:

We now uncover how we can express the characteristic energies
of the archer within our desired life design:

Meditate on these affirmations and then journal what you feel being brought
to attention within your own being. After journaling,
create your New Moon Design script for the Sagittarius New Moon.

I am defining my life passions & desires blissfully, exactly as I desire.
_____ is what sparks my curiosity.
_____ is what living a meaningful life means to me.
I am nurturing my faith & surrendering my urges to control
any & all outcomes, big or small.
I am connected to the right people, places & experiences in every moment,
I trust that.
My truth exposed & illuminated with bliss feels like this:

Beginning on the New Moon Dec. 6-10, 2018

CRESCENT MOON DATES: DEC. 11-14, 2018

FIRST QUARTER MOON DATES: DEC. 15-17, 2018

GIBBOUS MOON DATES: DEC. 18-21, 2018

FULL MOON DATES: DEC. 22-24, 2018

Full [cold] moon in Cancer, sun in Capricorn (opposite of Cancer)

DISSEMINATING MOON DATES: DEC. 25-28, 2018

THIRD QUARTER MOON DATES: DEC. 29-31, 2018

Finishing with the Balsamic Moon : Jan. 1-3, 2019

BECOMING YOUR BEST SELF
IS
SIMPLY
UNCOVERING
& EMBRACING
YOUR POTENTIAL
TO ALL THAT YOU ARE & DESIRE TO BE.

THE FOLLOWING DAILY JOURNALING PAGES ARE DESIGNED AS **DAILY** JOURNALING TOOLS.

THEY ARE UNIVERSAL AMONGST THE VARIOUS MOON PHASES & CYCLES OF THE YEAR.
FOLLOWING THESE PAGES DAILY ALLOWS FOR
ALIGNING, DESIGNING & MANIFESTING
ANY & ALL DESIRES.

THE I AM INFUSED WITH LOVE: PERSONAL ABUNDANCE JOURNAL BY ZAEYLIN SATYA
IS AVAILABLE FOR PURCHASE TO COMPLIMENT THE UTILIZATION OF THIS
MANIFESTING WITH THE MOON JOURNAL PROMPT GUIDE,
IT IS UNLINED & SIMPLY FOR THOSE WHO WOULD LIKE A MATCHING, SAME SIZE DESIGN TO CREATE IN.
IT IS SEPARATE FROM THIS DESIGNER GUIDEBOOK SO THAT IT IS NOT TAKING UP A LARGE PIECE OF THE
DESIGNER .. WHILE ALSO BEING FILLED IN A SHORT AMOUNT OF TIME. SINCE THE DESIGNER IS CREATED FOR
ONE YEAR USE, WE WOULD NEED QUITE A FEW EXTRA PAGES TO JOURNAL IN. THIS WAY YOUR GODDESS LIFE
DESIGNER STAYS CLEAN & FILLED ONLY WITH SIGNIFICANT TOOLS & REFERENCES FOR YOUR LIFE & YOUR
GOALS. YOU CAN PURCHASE THE MATCHING BLANK-PAGED JOURNAL AS OFTEN AS YOU FILL IT, OR YOU CAN
USE YOUR OWN FAVOURITE JOURNAL / JOURNALING METHOD. BE OPEN TO TRYING DIFFERENT METHODS.
YOUR POWERS OF MANIFESTING WILL INCREASE WHEN **YOU** ARE MOST COMFORTABLE ..
TRULY ENJOYING THE THINGS **YOU** ARE DOING EACH DAY --- JOURNALING INCLUDED.

THERE WILL BE A GODDESS LIFE DESIGNER FORMULATED FOR EACH COMING YEAR.

Goddess Life Designer

I NOW HAVE THE WISDOM & WRITTEN DESIGN PLAN NECESSARY FOR ME
TO TAKE ACTION ON MY PART.
THE UNIVERSE IS MEETING ME
& DOING ITS PART.
I AM GRATEFUL.

WHEN FEELING STUCK HANDLING A 'PROBLEM':

MY 'PROBLEM' IS _____.

IS THIS COMPLETELY OUT OF MY CONTROL?
IF YES, THEN I RELAX INTO EASE WITHIN MY FAITH IN THE DIVINE,
OR PERFORM A RITUAL TO SURRENDER.
IF NO, THEN MY IDEAL SOLUTION IS _____.
[IGNITE ALL SENSES INTO YOUR SOLUTION]

I CHOOSE TO LET GO WHEN I AM NOT IN CONTROL,
I TRUST THE UNIVERSE ALWAYS HAS MY BACK,
MAKING MOVES FOR ME EVEN WHEN I CANNOT SEE,
I AM CONFIDENTLY TRUSTING WHAT I CANNOT SEE.
I CHOOSE TO FOCUS ON THE FEELINGS OF MY IDEAL SOLUTION,
AS I HAVE FULL FAITH THAT
THE UNIVERSE IS SUPPORTING MY EVERY INTENTION I EMIT FROM MY BEING.
WHEN I MOVE, THE UNIVERSE MOVES WITH ME TO SUPPORT ME.
WHEN I HAVE DONE ALL I CAN DO,
I RELAX & HAVE FAITH THAT MY DIVINE, CREATIVE SOURCE LOVES ME
& IS TAKING CARE OF ME.

DREAM. LIVE. BE GRATEFUL. GIVE.

Morning Journaling ..

I AM GRATEFUL FOR AWAKENING THIS MORNING,

MY LIFETIME IS FILLED WITH & FUELED BY THE BLISSFUL EXPERIENCES OF MY OWN DEEPEST DESIRES FULFILLED.

I AM THRIVING WITHIN MY PASSIONATE HUMAN EXISTENCE.

BEFORE JOURNALING TAKE A MOMENT, OR A FEW, TO DO SOME BREATHING

OR MEDITATION YOU FEEL DRAWN TO.

CONNECT WITH YOUR HEARTBEAT, BREATH & INNER POWER.

I AM SO GRATEFUL FOR ..

1

2

3

4

5

♥ REFLECT ON THE CURRENT MOON PHASE'S PAGE ♥

TAKE 5 MINUTES TO BE STILL AND VISUALIZE THE IDEAL WAY YOUR DAY WILL UNFOLD.

I CHOOSE WHERE MY ENERGY GOES TODAY.

I INVITE ALL THINGS WONDERFUL INTO MY LIFE TODAY.

I CHOOSE MY THOUGHTS TODAY.

I CHOOSE TO EMBODY FAITH OVER FEAR IN EACH MOMENT OF THIS DAY.

I AM ALWAYS CONNECTED TO MY DIVINE LIFE SOURCE,
I AM THE EMBODIMENT OF INFINITE GODDESS POWER.

FOR EACH OF THE FOLLOWING PROMPTS:

HOW I AM FEELING// WHAT I APPRECIATE ABOUT MYSELF// DO I FEEL I AM WORTHY OF RECEIVING MY BEST DAY TODAY?// ALL THE THINGS I NEED TO LET GO OF IN ORDER TO MOVE FORWARD TODAY// I CAN DO THESE 3 THINGS TO BRING ME CLOSER TO MY GOAL TODAY// I ASK MY DIVINE SOURCE FOR GUIDANCE & SUPPORT IN THE AREA(S) OF MY CHOOSING, BECAUSE I KNOW MY SOURCE LOVES ENGAGEMENT FROM ME & ASSISTING ME WITH MY INSPIRATIONS, PASSIONS & DESIRES// MY IDEAL DAY IS ALIGNED WITH ME NOW, I AM SO GRATEFUL// THE VIBE I DESIRE TO BE TODAY// THE VIBE I DESIRE TO BE AROUND TODAY// THE MINDSET I DESIRE TO BE IN THROUGHOUT THIS DAY// MEDITATION NOTES// OTHER WRITING PROMPTS MY HIGHEST SELF IS PULLING ME TOWARDS// ANY PROMPT THE UNIVERSE IS NUDGING INTO MY VIEW THIS DAY.

ONLY 10% OF OUR LIFE IS DETERMINED BY OUR CIRCUMSTANCES,

THE REMAINING 90% IS DETERMINED BY

THE ATTITUDE WE PERSONALLY CHOOSE TO EMBODY

WHILE PERCEIVING AND REACTING TO THE CIRCUMSTANCES.

RECOGNIZE THIS & BE MINDFUL IN EACH & EVERY MOMENT OF LIFE.

~I PRACTICE VARIOUS FORMS OF SELF LOVE TODAY~

I FEEL AMAZING TODAY BY
THINKING ON THE THINGS I LOVE & APPRECIATE IN MY LIFE
AND BY DOING THINGS THAT MAKE ME FEEL TRULY AMAZING.
THIS RAISES MY VIBRATION, ACTING AS A VIBRATIONAL MAGNET
~~~ ATTRACTING MY DESIRES WITH EASE ~~~

I MOVE MY BODY BECAUSE I LOVE MY BODY.

I CELEBRATE ALL OF MY SUCCESSES BOTH BIG & SMALL!

I REFLECT ON THE WRITTEN DESIRES I AM MANIFESTING.
I GIVE THANKS IN ADVANCE FOR MY DESIRES ~
TRULY FEELING INTO HOW MY DESIRES WILL FEEL AS
A FULFILLED, PRESENT MOMENT FACT WITHIN MY LIFE.

I MEDITATE ON MY VISION BOARD DAILY.
I DO NOT VISUALIZE JUST TO MANIFEST,
I VISUALIZE TO KNOW THESE THINGS ARE ALREADY MINE,
TO KNOW (AND MOST IMPORTANTLY TO FEEL)
WITHIN MY BODY AND MIND THAT THEY ARE ALREADY MINE.
I MUST KNOW THIS AS TRUTH WITHIN MY MIND AND BODY FIRST,
THEY WILL PHYSICALLY MANIFEST SECOND, ONCE I HAVE FIRST
MASTERED FEELING & KNOWING THEY ARE ALREADY MINE.

I DESIRE WITH A PLAYFUL ATTITUDE
I LET GO OF WONDERING HOW AND WHEN MY DESIRES
WILL APPEAR. INSTEAD, I AM EXCITED TO SEE
HOW MY DIVINE SOURCE WILL WORK ITS MAGIC ~
IN BRINGING MY DESIRES TO ME AS I
MOVE FORWARD WITH INSPIRED ACTION.
~ ACTION ALONE IS 'DOING' IN ORDER TO MAKE SOMETHING
HAPPEN, INSPIRED ACTION IS
'DOING' WITH THE FEELINGS OF JOY & INSPIRATION,
FLOWING & ALLOWING THINGS TO HAPPEN ~

I WRITE MY INTUITIVE INSIGHTS DOWN AS I RECEIVE THEM,
TO RECALL & UTILIZE THEM WITHIN MY LIFE.

I DO NOT OBSESS OVER OUTCOMES I DESIRE, INSTEAD
I OBSESS OVER THE GOOD FEELINGS MY DESIRES COMPLETE,
MANIFESTED FORM BRINGS INTO MY LIFE.
I MEDITATE ON EXACTLY HOW THIS FEELS,
THIS IS HOW I HOLD FAITH WHILE
DETACHING & ALLOWING ~
I PRACTICE THE ART OF SURRENDER.
I AM THE EMBODIMENT OF FAITH.

I AM WHOLE, LOVE & LOVED.
I TREAT MY TEMPLE WELL
& NURTURE MY SOUL.
I AM GENTLE WITH MYSELF.

LIVE THIS DAY AS IF IT WERE YOUR LAST. THE PAST IS GONE & THE FUTURE IS NOT GUARANTEED.
-WAYNE DYER.
I AM PERFECTLY GUIDED IN EACH MOMENT OF MY LIFE JOURNEY.

GODDESS,

RELAXING INTO THE END OF THE DAY,
REFLECT ON & JOURNAL THESE PROMPTS:

BEFORE JOURNALING TAKE A MOMENT, OR A FEW,

TO DO SOME BREATHING OR MEDITATION YOU FEEL DRAWN TO.

CONNECT WITH YOUR HEARTBEAT, BREATH & INNER POWER.

I AM GRATEFUL THIS DAY HAS BROUGHT ME ..

1

2

3

TOMORROW I CAN ___ TO BOOST MY PRODUCTIVITY, SELF LOVE & ALIGNMENT WITH THE UNIVERSE.

MY DIVINE SOURCE OF POWER & LIFE IS ALWAYS SUPPORTING ME & MY DESIRED LIFE DESIGN.

HOW I LOVED MYSELF TODAY:

WHAT MAKES ME FEEL BEST ABOUT TODAY:

I BREATHE HEALING ENERGY INTO MY BODY,
I EXHALE ALL THAT DOES NOT SERVE MY HIGHEST SELF.
REPEAT.

I CUT ALL NEGATIVE ENERGY CORDS, I FOCUS ON MYSELF & MINDING MY OWN BUSINESS.
I WELCOME INTUITIVE INSIGHTS & INSPIRATION WITHIN MY NIGHTLY DREAMS.
WHATEVER MINDSET I AM IN AS I FALL ASLEEP CREATES
THE FREQUENCY OF DREAM I WILL EXPERIENCE.
WHILE ASLEEP I AM MARINATING IN MY SUBCONSCIOUS MIND.
I AM MINDFUL IN ELEVATING MY VIBRATIONAL FREQUENCY 5-10 MINUTES BEFORE &
ALL THE WAY INTO FALLING SLEEP.
DOING SO IS VERY EFFECTIVE IN PROGRAMMING MY SUBCONSCIOUS MIND
TO SUPPORT THE MANIFESTATION OF MY DESIRED LIFE DESIGN.
I MEDITATE ON THE VIBRATIONAL EMBODIMENT I WILL FEEL
WITH THE FULFILLMENT OF MY DESIRED LIFE DESIGN IS A PRESENT MOMENT FACT.

I GIVE THANKS.
I AM ALWAYS DIVINELY GUIDED.
I AM SAFE. I AM PROTECTED. I AM INFINITE. I AM ABUNDANT. I AM BLISSFUL. I AM BEAUTIFUL.

THE GODDESS LIFE DESIGNER
DAILY TO-DO LIST:

REFLECT ON THE CURRENT MOON PHASE'S PAGE.
[TO KNOW THE CURRENT MOON PHASE SIMPLY REFLECT ON
THE DETAILED PAGE FOR THE MOON CYCLE WE ARE IN, EACH
MOON CYCLE PAGE CONTAINS THE DATES FOR WHEN EACH
PHASE OCCURS DURING THAT SPECIFIC CYCLE]

↓

REFLECT ON THE MORNING JOURNALING PAGES

↓

REFLECT ON ANY OTHER PAGES / EXERCISES
YOU DESIRE TO THROUGHOUT YOUR DAY

↓

REFLECT ON THE END OF DAY JOURNALING PAGE

BLESSINGS ARE ALWAYS ALIGNED WITH YOU AND YOUR CREATIVE JOURNEY ♥

ALL OF THE THINGS I AM GRATEFUL FOR IN LIFE:

[ONE] OF THE PRINCIPAL REASONS WHY SO MANY FAIL TO GET WHAT THEY WANT IS BECAUSE
THEY DO NOT DEFINITELY KNOW WHAT THEY WANT, OR BECAUSE THEY CHANGE THEIR WANTS ALMOST EVERY DAY.
'KNOW WHAT YOU WANT AND CONTINUE TO WANT IT. YOU WILL GET IT IF YOU COMBINE DESIRE WITH FAITH.
THE POWER OF DESIRE WHEN COMBINED WITH FAITH BECOMES INVINCIBLE.'
- CHRISTIAN D. LARSON (1874-1954) YOUR FORCES AND HOW TO USE THEM

IF ONE ADVANCES CONFIDENTLY IN THE DIRECTION OF THEIR DREAMS, AND ENDEAVORS TO LIVE THE LIFE
WHICH THEY HAVE IMAGINED, THEY WILL MEET WITH A SUCCESS UNEXPECTED IN COMMON HOURS.
- HENRY DAVID THOREAU

I GIVE THANKS IN ADVANCE EVERY SINGLE DAY FOR ALL OF THE THINGS I DESIRE IN MY LIFE.
MY ULTIMATE LIFE DESIRES LISTED:

MY DAYDREAM/ DAILY THINKING IS A PREVIEW OF MY FUTURE REALITY.
I CHOOSE TO BE MINDFUL
IN ONLY THINKING AND DREAMING
ON THE THOUGHTS THAT PRODUCE THE FEELINGS I DESIRE TO MANIFEST AS MY REALITY.

SIMPLE DAILY PRAYER/MEDITATION/AFFIRMATION SCRIPT

I AM THANKFUL FOR _____.

FILL IN THE BLANK WITH EACH DESIRE YOU ARE MANIFESTING.

I TRUST THAT MY DIVINE SOURCE IS PROVIDING ME WITH EXACTLY WHAT I NEED
IN EACH MOMENT OF THIS LIFETIME.

I AM
WORTHY,
LOVE
&
LOVED.

THE REASONS WHY I LOVE & APPRECIATE MYSELF:

I AM CONSTANTLY GROWING, AND THAT IS BEAUTIFUL.

THERE IS NO 'FINAL DESTINATION' I AM GOING TO ONE DAY FIND MYSELF AT.

MY HAPPINESS AND SUCCESS RESIDE WITHIN MY PASSIONATE AND FULFILLING LIFE JOURNEY.

MY JOURNEY TAKES FORM EXACTLY AS I DESIRE,

BECAUSE I AM ALWAYS IN THE BLISSFUL MINDSET OF EXPERIENCING THE GRATITUDE

THAT COMES WITH MY DESIRES FULFILLED.

REFLECT ON THE EXPERIENCES YOU DESIRE TO HAVE IN YOUR LIFETIME--

ARE YOU GROWING IN THAT DIRECTION?

WHAT CAN YOU DO TO NOURISH YOUR GROWTH IN THAT DIRECTION?

'YOU ARE THE AVERAGE OF THE 5 PEOPLE YOU SPEND THE MOST TIME WITH'

RECOGNIZE THAT IN THIS PRESENT DAY AND AGE YOU HAVE THE POWER TO DEFINE THESE 5 PEOPLE

BY NON-PHYSICAL MEANS.

FOR EXAMPLE: YOUTUBE, AUDIBLE, SOCIAL MEDIA .. ETC

THEY ARE THE 5 PEOPLE YOU RESONATE WITH THE MOST ..

THE PEOPLE WHOSE ENERGY YOU DESIRE TO FILL YOUR MIND & YOUR TIME WITH.

Universal guidance to follow:

CHOOSE YOUR SEED.
BE CERTAIN OF WHAT YOU WANT. ORANGES CANNOT GROW FROM LEMON SEEDS. DON'T EXPECT THEM TO.

CHOOSE YOUR *desired life design.*
BE CERTAIN WITH YOURSELF ON WHAT IT IS YOU TRULY WANT.
USE DETAIL.

↓

PLANT YOUR SEED IN THE SOIL.
YOU KNOW WHICH PLANT YOUR SEED WILL GROW INTO,
BECAUSE YOU TOOK TIME TO CHOOSE IT YOURSELF.

PLANT YOUR IDEAL LIFE IN YOUR MIND.
KNOW THE DETAILS OF YOUR DESIRED LIFE DESIGN,
YOU ARE CERTAIN THIS IS WHAT YOU ARE GROWING WITHIN YOUR LIFE,
BECAUSE YOU TOOK TIME TO CHOOSE AND DEFINE YOUR LIFE AS YOU DESIRE IT TO BE.

↓

Water your seed.

Take inspired action towards, and in line with, your life design you desire.

↓

PROVIDE SUNLIGHT TO YOUR SEED.

DAYDREAM ON THE FEELINGS OF YOUR DESIRED LIFE DESIGN AS AN ALREADY ACHIEVED FACT.
GET FAMILIAR WITH THESE FEELINGS, ALWAYS FEEL THEM IN ORDER TO STAY INSPIRED.
POSITIVE FEELINGS FUEL GROWTH.
BY FEELING ANY DOUBT OR FEELINGS OF LACK YOU ARE SELF-SABOTAGING YOUR GARDEN
BY PLANTING AND GIVING ALL OF THE AVAILABLE SUNLIGHT TO NUMEROUS WEEDS.
THE WEEDS WILL GROW PROMINENTLY, FUELED BY YOUR NEGATIVE FEELINGS OF... THEM.
WITH ALL OF THESE WEEDS YOUR CHOSEN SEED WILL EITHER STRUGGLE TO GROW,
OR SIMPLY NOT GROW AT ALL.
FEELINGS OF DOUBT, LACK AND DWELLING ON ALL THAT COULD POSSIBLY GO WRONG ARE
THE WEEDS OF YOUR GARDEN.
IT IS CRUCIAL TO FOCUS ON WHAT YOU ARE STRIVING TOWARDS.
FEEL THE POSITIVE FEELINGS ASSOCIATED WITH THAT.

↓

NOW YOU CAN GROW YOUR DESIRED LIFE DESIGN SUCCESSFULLY INTO BLOSSOMING FORM.
ALLOW THE WATER + SUNLIGHT PROCESS TO REPEAT AND BECOME YOUR EVERY MOMENT STATE OF
BEING THROUGHOUT EACH DAY. THEN,
YOUR DESIRED LIFE DESIGN WILL BEGIN TO TAKE FULL BLOSSOM BEFORE YOUR EYES.

Love The Goddess Life Designer?

Inspire others via review &
share your feedback with me~

Are there any potential additions / alterations you would love to see?

IG: I check in periodically~ I post inspiration / recommendations I am feeling.
@zaeylinsatya

The eBook version is also available for purchase on Amazon.

The 2019 version will be available in November 2018.

Study your personal natal birth chart here:
http://astro.cafeastrology.com/natal.php

Blessings to you and your creative journey.